"One is thus led to ask whether schools of education are capable of coordination in the university with such professions as law and medicine. The American teachers college has not yet proved the affirmative. And it seems on the whole less impressive at the moment than when it was proposed a generation ago."

Abraham Flexner, *Universities: American, English, German* (1930)

American Graduate Schools of Education

A View from Abroad

A Report to the Ford Foundation
by Harry Judge

One of a series of reports on activities supported by the Ford
Foundation. A complete list of publications may be obtained
from the Ford Foundation Office of Reports, 320 East 43
Street, New York, New York 10017.

Library of Congress Cataloging in Publication Data
Judge, Harry George.
    American graduate schools of education.

    "A report to the Ford Foundation."
    1. Education — United States — Graduate work. I. Ford
Foundation. II. Title.
LB2372.E3J8   1982   378'.1553'0973   82-11076
ISBN 0-916584-21-6   AACR2

Contents

Preface

In 1977, several foundations, including the Ford Foundation, supported meetings of the presidents of fifteen leading research universities in the United States to address collectively the relationship of their institutions and services to the national interest, and the consequent responsibilities of the federal government with regard to such institutions. One outcome of these meetings was a report published later that year, entitled *Research Universities and the National Interest*. It speaks of the role of research universities in the United States as they contribute to the nation's well-being, both today and in the future. Further, it offers recommendations for strengthening them in order to ensure their capacity to continue to serve.

One of the many areas in which these universities play an important role is that of education itself. In almost all the research universities in the United States, there are faculties and programs that deal specifically with the policies, practice, and profession of education. These universities often support undergraduate and graduate schools or colleges of education; still others support departments of education. In virtually all of them, the emphasis is on research about learning, teaching, and education in general. Within some, the emphasis is on training people for work in the profession of education, most often in the public schools and in related agencies.

It was within this context—the American research university and its school or department of education — that the Ford Foundation asked Dr. Harry G. Judge of Oxford University, in England, a historian by training and an educational leader by experience, to conduct a series of visits at a sample of such schools and departments in U.S. research universities and exchange views with the people working in them or who are served by them. Broadly speaking, his purpose was to address the question: What is the place and role of the school of education in the research university, particularly at the graduate level, as well as in the world of educational practice itself? No hard and fixed boundaries were drawn for defining these schools and universities, for drawing up a scientific sample of them, or for developing a highly structured way of looking at them. As for the world of practice, we asked Doctor Judge to assume that the primary place of practice is in America's public schools and school systems, specifically, the practice of the professionals who staff them.

In brief, the assignment was to get the impressions and views of a thoughtful and collegial "outsider" who himself, as director of the Department of Educational Studies at Oxford University, must face the issue personally and professionally in that context. Our hope is that Doctor Judge's writings about his sojourn in this universe of institutions will be enlightening and provocative to those in this country who serve and lead education schools and who otherwise have some responsibility for them.

To introduce Doctor Judge's book to the American public, we asked Harold Howe II, currently a faculty member at a graduate school of education and formerly vice-president for education and public policy at the Ford Foundation, U.S. Commissioner of Education, a school administrator, and a teacher, to write the following foreword.

Edward J. Meade, Jr.
Ford Foundation

Foreword

Harry Judge's essay about graduate schools (departments) of education at major research universities in the United States is not designed to make the inhabitants of such schools or departments comfortable. Some will criticize his methods and some his conclusions.

But Doctor Judge, chairman of Oxford University's education department, is a friendly and discerning critic and observer, and a disarming one as well. In Chapter VII he uses a device that adds both charm and depth to the observations presented in Chapters I through VI; in that final chapter, he yields the floor to the imaginary American professor of education Benedict Rosencrantz, who, as a composite of the several able scholars of American education among whom Doctor Judge circulated his six chapters in final draft, proceeds to attempt the demolition of the views presented in Doctor Judge's ''own'' chapters!

The central finding of Doctor Judge's study is a paradox. On one hand, the scholars and teachers of education in our major graduate schools are seen as first-rate in both research and instruction; on the other hand, they are viewed as second-rate in these areas by their colleagues in the rest of the university — and sometimes by themselves. Doctor Judge wonders why this paradox should obtain, particularly in a country with the greatest and most pervasive commitment to education in all its forms of any other in the world.

I do not question this central paradox. Not only have I heard it in off-the-record conversations for many years, but I also accept that he heard it and that he has reported it directly and honestly. Harry Judge is telling us something that needs to be brought out in the open, and in doing so he does a service to those American universities where education is a serious topic. Put boldly, he has politely and firmly identified one of the persistent snobberies of academia in the United States.

Harry Judge's discussion of this phenomenon is not his only contribution in this short volume. Again and again, he provides that important ingredient we are so frequently denied: the capacity to see ourselves as others see us. Whether they are right or wrong, our thinking about ourselves is enriched.

My own view of Harry Judge's paradox is less complex than his, and is probably simplistic. I'll let him speak for himself and make my case briefly. I think that really first-class scholarship and analysis and teaching about education in the United States is not valued as much in universities as are similar activities in other fields mainly for three reasons. The first reason is that the plethora of graduate work in education in this country has produced a vast outpouring of second- and third-class work, some in universities with otherwise high standards. This overwhelming body of mediocrity casts its shadow on the truly excellent work going forward in some places, including those visited by Doctor Judge. Those who fail to see the spots of brightness always present within the shadow commit the same error as any critic engaging in generalization without identifying important exceptions.

The second reason is that education in America, in all its ramifications and diversity, is necessarily a confused subject. We all have a tendency to talk about ''American education'' as if it were discussable. It is not. Before discussion can have focus and meaning, American education must be broken down into its constituent parts. Our nonsystem of private and public education defies simplistic understanding because of its diversity, which is also its greatest strength. Sadly, this state of affairs often eludes the privileged people who dwell in a corner of that nonsystem — the academic departments of major research universities. Too easily, they tend to view education as a feeder system that produces the students they want produced, and not much else. This failing lies at the root of some of the snobbery in universities toward the study of education, which is often focused upon students and issues unrelated to the concerns of most research university professors.

Third, much of the concern about education in graduate schools of education touches one aspect or another of the nation's public schools, including that of preparing teachers and administrators for those schools. It is widely known in academia that, generally, those teachers and administrators score lower in the graduate record exam (G.R.E.) and other measures of scholarly talent than do aspirants for the Ph.D. in, say, physics or the professional degrees in law and medicine. This knowledge easily translates into second-class citizenship at universities for students of education and for their professors, whether or not those professors deserve such a label because of their research and teaching and whether or not the G.R.E. is, in fact, the ideal instrument for finding the right people to do the daily work of the schools. In addition, the long history of America's declared belief in education, paralleled by a history of discrimination against women and minorities and economic discrimination against teachers, is forgotten as a set of circumstances to be considered when such judgments are made.

It is as important to ventilate the problems, the achievements, and the shortcomings of those who engage in the serious study of education as it is for those in such other major fields as law, business, and engineering. Our society and its economy depend on a constant process of criticism and improvement growing out of such an exercise. Harry Judge has done us all a service in bringing to that process of ventilation some assertions and reports that all too often are left out of the discussion because they aren't considered polite or because they trouble the egos of the education professional.

Harold Howe II
Senior Lecturer
Harvard Graduate School of Education

CHAPTER I

The Human Factor

This short book is about the place of the graduate schools of education in research universities in the United States. For the reader who is not an American, I must therefore explain that the research universities constitute the most prestigious sector of higher education and are characterised by an emphasis upon graduate work measured by the conferment of the doctor's degree. Within them, the graduate schools of education are professional and research schools, concentrating upon the award of higher degrees in education. For the most part, they no longer see themselves as deeply concerned with the training of teachers.

The form of this book is that of an essay followed by a letter, both of which are concerned with the discussion of a puzzle. That puzzle, which I shall unpack later in this chapter, revolves around the question of why graduate schools of education, many of international renown, occupy so unclear and uncomfortable a position, both in the world of the research universities and in other fields.

I willingly undertook the writing of this book at the invitation of the Ford Foundation. The senior officials of the foundation are busy people, so I was delighted but not surprised to receive a telephone call from Edward J. Meade, Jr., of the Ford Foundation in the summer of 1978 proposing a brisk meeting at Heathrow Airport. We met and talked, for neither the first nor the last time, by a barely credible Caribbean pool in an airport hotel, the style of which has been caught in an episode of Graham Greene's *The Human Factor*.

Ed Meade, programme officer in the Division of Education and Public Policy, was no stranger to England and its ways, nor yet to Oxford. His proposal, as it took shape at an earlier meeting of the National Academy of Education, was that an Englishman with appropriate interests but no previous involvement should look at several graduate schools of education in American research universities with a view to speaking about them or, more properly, about the issues and questions that might be provoked by visiting them. The proposal was later enlarged so that during 1980 as well, but on an even more restricted basis of time, some of the visits made in 1979 could be repeated and others could be added.

This was, therefore, a small-scale operation. In all, I visited some ten universities and spent about sixteen weeks in the United States. In my bad moments I was inevitably reminded of such uncomfortable precedents or warnings as, for example, 'Most novels about Oxford are written by elderly ladies on the strength of three days spent in Cambridge twenty years ago.' Friends anxious, for whatever reason, to reassure me insist that no-one else has spent so long looking at this particular problem, or even tried to discover if there is one, or had easy access to so many distinguished institutions in so short a time. It must, indeed, be the case (in the States, as elsewhere, but perhaps especially there) that most professors' view of a place other than their own is based on a mixture of stereotyping, folklore, gossip (sometimes amiably malicious), report by interested or offended parties, knowledge of a few distinguished scholars and their published work, and recollections of a different age when they were 'there' themselves.

A few words on my method of working will also be helpful in laying bare the basis of the comments and observations with which this book is sprinkled. I tried to avoid short or fragmented visits, instead attempting in each place (with uneven success) to acquire some sense of locality and style. It quickly became obvious, for example, that the nature of the particular university, and the way in which, formally and informally, it distributed esteem were, if not determinants of then certainly limitations upon, what a particular school of education could achieve or even attempt.

I shall not forget the generosity of the deans and others in sharing not only their time but also their thoughts. On each visit I spent time with a dean and the dean's colleagues, faculty members over as wide a range as possible, and students. On many visits I spoke at length with the president or some representative of the administration. At several universities, as a result of both personal contacts and formal enquiries, I spent time with members of different graduate schools, as well as members of undergraduate schools.

During one autumnal month I indulged to the full my taste for stability and my sense that the issues after which I was stumbling could be studied only in context. I therefore anchored myself in one university and diversified my days (not that they were in any way tedious) by occasional cruises from the academic harbour to the surrounding capes and islands of professional and educational life. In this way I could talk and (much more important) listen at length and within a shared context at other schools of the same university, at a local state college, in the offices of superintendents and representatives of teachers' unions, in the classrooms, corridors, and staff lounges of a secondary school lying only a few hundred yards from the university itself. In Washington I spoke with some of those who run the world, cause it to be run, or stop its running.

It was obvious from the beginning that keeping track of five or six intensive conversations every day would not be easy. Thus, I was never without a note-book in my pocket, and at the end of every few days, I wrote several pages of my chronicle. This was worked into typescript in five instalments which, when duly bound together, constitute the unpublished Appendix of this book.

At the end of each visit, I wrote what I deliberately called, and call, an 'essay,' which essentially was a raw version of Chapters II-VI of this book. After preliminary consultation, the text was sent to a wide cross-section of those I had already visited and from whom I had learnt so much. Each recipient agreed to welcome me again, some six weeks after receiving the preliminary text, in order to comment on and propose changes in the draft. For me, that was something of an un-nerving experience, but it had the effect of persuading me that, with certain important reservations, I had produced a serviceable analysis of the problem. I have kept a careful record of all these conversations. Several of those who reviewed the drafts also wrote letters and memoranda about them.

When I returned to England, I brooded on the comments I had received and made two decisions. The first decision, which was easy and obvious enough, was to incorporate in the early chapters the corrections of fact or judgement that had been proposed to me. But that did not dispose of a major criticism. I was told that, by stopping the text at the end of Chapter VI, I was guilty of leaving the subject and the reader up in the air.

At the same time, I had no intention of offering easy, cheerful solutions to what I saw as a complex, distinctively American problem. For that reason, I made the second decision. I took an outrageous liberty with my friends, conflated them into one American wise man, and caused him to write me 'A Letter from America'. There is nothing, nothing at all, in Chapter VII that was not said to me on more than one occasion by those I talked to. I claim it, therefore, as fiction based upon careful listening and analysis.

3

One paragraph should be sufficient to explain my prejudices and background. Throughout most of my life I have worked in secondary schools in England. At one such school (Banbury, in Oxfordshire), I was deeply engaged as the principal in the reorganisation of schools along comprehensive lines, a reorganisation that was so prominent a feature of the 1960's. At the same time, I was a member of the Labour Government's Public Schools Commission, which addressed the nature of the relationship between the public and private sectors of education. I was later asked to report on teacher education in Britain, and for a year I served full-time on the Committee of Inquiry under the chairmanship of Lord James of Rusholme. Shortly afterwards, I became director of the Department of Educational Studies at Oxford University. In that capacity, I was concerned to consolidate and develop the natural relationships of the university with the world of schooling and of the department (in effect, by American standards, a small graduate school) with the university at large.

This, then, is the 'I' who was invited to undertake the task I described above — namely, the exploration of a puzzle, which I must now attempt to describe more fully.

There is no country in the world in which education occupies a more important place than it does in the United States. The newspapers are full of it, and not only of comment or information of a pessimistic or woeful kind (although there is no shortage of that). It is, arguably, the largest national industry. Education, organised as a schooling activity, is expected to resolve, or at least to ameliorate, a bewildering range of social and economic problems.

There is, therefore, nothing inherently surprising in the scale and importance of higher education in the United States. Participation in it persists, with surprising steadiness, at an outstandingly high level. American universities, at their best, embody the highest international standards of scholarship, and many justly enjoy glittering prestige. Universities and colleges are arranged, or they arrange themselves, in a series of flexible hierarchies of function and esteem. Within these universities — and especially within the score or so that evoke an admiring nod of recognition in Sydney, Paris, Rome, or London — graduate schools represent the highest, most enviable peak of achievement and recognition.

Graduate schools themselves are divided into different, though not always accurately definable, categories. Some, such as the graduate schools of arts and sciences, have adopted ideals of scholarship and research. They are the homes of many men and women of national and scholarly repute. To them are attracted the product of the nation's universities and colleges. They nurture Ph.D.'s of quality and by the thousands. Their products aspire to tenured posts in places of higher education — the best in the best. They are the principal recipients of research grants from the federal government and foundations.

Alongside such graduate schools of arts and sciences in most American research universities stand the graduate professional schools of medicine, law, or business, to name a few prominent categories. Only the graduate schools of medicine are, in nature and function, matched by corresponding institutions in Europe. To these graduate schools come some of the ablest and most ambitious of aspiring professionals. By hard work and the investment of hard cash they secure degrees — not the Ph.D. — which, when conferred by the right schools, earn them advancement, prestige, and money.

Within this second type of graduate school, the professional school, and enclosed by the most charmed inner circle of the very best universities, is found not more than a score of graduate schools of education. They may carry responsibilities for undergraduates (a point certainly requiring further examination), but they perceive themselves as, and wish to be described as, 'graduate schools'.

This small group of graduate schools of education is lodged securely at the heart of another network. They and the scholars whose presence graces them enjoy high esteem among both their peers and their inferiors — it is certain that they have no superiors — in the international business of Education (dignified with a capital E). They enjoy a similarly high visibility, not always unaccompanied by a hint of resentment or rancour, among schools and colleges of education in the United States as a whole. We all know which ones they are.

So far, there is no more than the barest hint of an emerging puzzle. Education and schooling are of central importance in and to the United States. Higher education is rich and elaborate; within its generous structures there flourish research universities endowed with powerful graduate schools. Among these graduate schools are some schools of education, which bask in national and international favour. Moreover, and to close the circle before opening the puzzle, it is these very graduate schools that are related (are they not?) to the education and schooling which, it is agreed, are of central importance in and to the United States. Thus, their place should be assured, unassailable.

For me, the puzzle is that this apparently unavoidable conclusion simply does not follow. On the contrary, graduate schools of education display alarming symptoms of insecurity and self-doubt. They know that their position within the world of higher education, and often within their parent universities, is always ambiguous and often resented. Their leading members are not sure whether they are — or wish to be — part of a graduate school of arts and sciences or of a professional school. By deliberate choice, they have tended to distance themselves from both the task of training teachers for elementary and secondary schools and that of addressing the problems and needs of those schools. Practitioners (teachers and administrators) in the very fields they are, in principle, intended to cultivate all too often dismiss the fields as remote and their work as irrelevant. Deep discomforts of this kind were perhaps hidden in the decades of prosperity and growth. They are becoming only too painfully obvious as money for research and development dries up or is diverted elsewhere, as enrolments are threatened, as the higher education system as a whole comes under growing economic pressure and public questioning. Let there be no doubt about one thing: the scholars who work in the places that puzzle me are without rivals, both in the quality of their work and in the openness and generosity with which they were prepared to discuss the nature and causes of the institutional doubt with which I became, as the months went by, increasingly preoccupied. The quality of these men and women, rather, serves to deepen the puzzle, which might now be restated somewhat as follows. Why should famous graduate schools, apparently central to so much in American public and academic life, be regarded as, and regard themselves as, peripheral, as insecure, as undeserving of esteem? Why, in all these respects and at the risk of simplifying the puzzle to the point of dissolution, are they so unlike, for example, law schools?

So much for the puzzle. My attempt to discuss it was originally called an "essay," and for a number of good reasons. I am not myself (whatever Professor Benedict Rosencrantz may himself choose to write in the last chapter) in the business of making recommendations or offering prescriptions. That would be impertinent and foolish. Nor is an essayist, as distinct from a social scientist (which I am not) expected to be immaculately objective and impersonal; that is why I have taken some trouble to describe my own perspective. Nor can the reader legitimately expect completeness and finality. Glanville defined an essay as an 'incomplete offer at a subject'. I am convinced that the subject of this essay/book is both important and urgent. My warmest hope is that others will take it up — others, that is, with greater knowledge and resources.

If this essay is not inspired by a spirit of general criticism, still less is it to be taken as commentary on a specific place or specific places. In the next two chapters I shall, indeed, invent two such places. It will then be clear that my interest throughout is in issues and questions, not in local circumstances *per se* (seductively fascinating as they must always be to the historian or the chronicler). Of course, I went to Chicago, Stanford, and Harvard, to UCLA, Ohio State, and Illinois, and to Teachers' College, Columbia. And I went to other places simply because they were not on the lips of *cognoscenti*. In each place the people I met talked about the other places; they had often been on the faculty of one or more of them. What slowly grew in my mind was a pattern of underlying dilemmas, and not a set of portraits, whether friendly or hostile. It would be insulting for me to express an opinion on institutions as distinct from issues; I hope I have avoided doing so.

It is time to offer the material for the analysis that follows. This material is presented in a form of which Rosencrantz proves to be very critical — as, naturally, were many but by no means all of my friends who read these chapters in draft. The form is one of imaginary portraits of two universities. They are, of course, composite portraits which permit me to draw out the underlying structural characteristics of many of the great graduate schools of education. A critic who wishes to dismiss them, who believes that all is well in those schools and that their faculties are confident and assured, is therefore offered a perfect alibi for doing so. 'These places do not exist', he will argue, and he will be right. My reply must be that there is in these two chapters not one fact or observation that is unrecorded in my chronicle, nor one character or quotation that cannot be readily found in those same pages.

And so to Waterend. . . .

CHAPTER II

Waterend

Waterend is a private university with a long history. It now sits, although that is altogether too reposeful a verb, secure on one of the commanding peaks of higher education. Waterend is respectful towards, even proud of, its undergraduate education, but the self-defining purposes of the place find expression in the rich range of its graduate schools: arts and sciences, law, business, medicine. It has a school neither of journalism nor of dentistry.

In conversation, the president declares himself unsure as to whether his university would in the 1980's create a school of education. Since, however, it has had something of the kind for nearly a century, and because the president's agenda is a crowded one, the question seems hardly worth pursuing. The school of education, relatively small and within its sector highly prestigious, indubitably does exist; thus the important questions turn rather on its evolution, present purposes, and future tasks. Nevertheless, some on campus presume to ask, even of the Waterend School of Education, whether the university as a whole does itself much good by remaining in so uncertain and vulnerable a business.

Within the school itself, such doubts find some echoes, often heard as anxieties. The school, like many others (and to an extent that surprises many English visitors), is highly conscious and justifiably proud of its history. Several decades ago, under the guidance of a brilliant and determined dean, the School of Education began to distance itself from the confused and unattractive world of teacher education. But its climb to a purer form of academic respectability seems now to be interrupted, even threatened. Although it has long since abstracted itself from teacher training and has successfully aligned itself with many of the standards of arts and sciences (rather than of the professional schools), its confidence is affected indirectly by the declining demand for teachers and therefore for those who lead or prepare them, whether in administration or scholarship. The university as a whole faces financial problems of unprecedented difficulty, and hardly any activity goes unexamined.

There is, moreover, a corrosive sense in the air that the great days are almost certainly over. An entire generation of names familiar in many if not quite all American households is drawing to its appointed close. The litany of names recalls the lines from *Punch,* in 1893: 'Nearly all our best men are dead! Carlyle, Tennyson, Browning, George Eliot! — I'm not feeling very well myself'.

Yet the flame of the school's mission burns as brightly as ever. The school is in the business of *studying* education, for there is no other way to flourish in such places as this. Above all, its leaders should create new knowledge. The assumption, tested in a range of conversations, is that in only a few places can this standard of creativity be maintained, and then only at some distance from the mess and hurly-burly of the environment of a typical university.

The faculty are not unduly preoccupied with questions of careers for their doctoral students — and these are the ones that count. In the past, at any rate, their graduates have had little cause for concern. Many are from overseas, and many return there. Others have moved purposefully up the career ladders of administration. Many more, marching to the insistent drumbeat of Waterend, have sought and found academic preferment in the universities, even occasionally finding appointments (as sociologists, for example) in what are revealingly called 'mainstream departments'. Things are by no means as easy as they were, however. Enrolments are declining, there is concern about standards, a disturbingly large amount of teaching must be undertaken in the early evening or on week-ends.

The School's days of expansion were marked, especially under the inspiration of Dean Strong, by a clear and occasionally ruthless policy of hiring and firing. The dominant tactic was to make a foray into the disciplines, to track down a scholar of achieved distinction or of sparkling promise, and to carry him triumphantly through the gates of Waterend. Thereafter, the professor would be careful to explain that this was the first appointment he had ever held in a school of education, that he was unsullied by contact with the lower worlds of educational practice, that he was first and foremost a Waterend Professor — with at least a courtesy appointment in another department as well.

Given the nature of the academic world in general and such a place as Waterend in particular, such a professor is unlikely to be concerned primarily with the only too visible problems of schools and schooling. Why should he be? — especially as he may hold the reasonable conviction that not much (save by way of first-aid interventions) can, in any case, be done by research universities to address those problems.

Instead, the professor turns — or more precisely, *remains* turned, according to his tastes and his discipline — towards such questions as the history of the family, the rôle of the media in the formation of public opinion, the structure of higher education, the changing shape of macro-economics, or the evolution of organisational theory. In all these areas, his constituency of first resort continues to comprise scholars within the discipline that formed him and in which he must excel.

Excellent work is therefore done, but a price is paid. Many of those who make that particular pilgrimage — *from* psychology *to* education, for example — have divided hearts and minds. The joint appointment is perceived as an accolade conferred by a reigning discipline upon a dependent activity. The migrant doubts whether he can satisfy at one and the same time both the constituency he left and the more vaguely delimited one he has joined. He may welcome the imposition upon him of the requirements of applicability and relevance (while wondering 'To what?'), yet regret (or even resent) the fact that his present brethren in psychology have much more time for research.

It is certain that a psychologist (or sociologist or economist) in the Waterend School of Education will have to address his mind not only to research but also to teaching and students. Many of these students (of whom, at Waterend and elsewhere, more must be said later) will be in pursuit of the Ed.D. The professor himself is much more likely to hold the Ph.D. The difference of two letters may symbolise a problem that is largely peculiar to such schools of education.

Waterend is a private university. Although it is a rich one, it needs students to provide tuition (*fees,* in the English context). Many of these students have fairly precise objectives, which have a bearing upon careers in education. That is to say, their objectives are professional. Only a minority — certainly in the 1980's — can expect, or be encouraged to hope, that an academic career is accessible. The match between the needs and expectations of such students and the intentions of the faculty may therefore be less than perfect.

Several consequences follow, particularly at Waterend but elsewhere as well. Professors back briskly away from any suggestion that they are in the business of 'training'. They show signs of uneasiness if their courses are linked to concepts of credentialling or licensing. 'Our courses do not enable a successful student to hang up a shingle'. What they, as professors, are concerned to do is to develop skills of thinking and analysis, not perfect a knowledge of budgeting techniques or legislative and procedural niceties.

Like most of the places with which it may in whole or in part be compared, Waterend has changed in this respect since the early tenure of Dean Strong. Alongside a powerful scholarly orientation, it once celebrated an active interest in the business of school superintendency. It supported – or, more honestly, allowed others to support – a strong regional centre for educational organisation and management. One of the most prominent of its faculty devoted much time and energy to developing such courses and even more to recruiting bright students, placing successful ones, and systematically cultivating influential *alumni*.

The School was larger then, education was booming, and it was at once desirable and relatively easy to pursue objectives that may well have been compatible but that were *not* identical. In such areas as the administration of higher education (a large training enterprise that does not exist in Europe), two tracks could comfortably be maintained. Down one track, towards the beckoning Ph.D., travelled the minority, of whom much was required and to whom much was given by the professors Dean Strong had imported. Down the other, and assuredly less demanding track, towards the Ed.D., travelled a multitude who required (and asked for) less careful nurturing. Of course, the multitude paid for the minority, but there would be no good reason for complaining about that.

Contraction has now folded the two tracks into one, so that there is no longer a stream of students bound for research and academic appointments and another (amounting to a flood) directed towards appointments in educational administration. Research and service functions have become confused within one programme, and restraints of staffing have generated attempts to discharge both functions at one and the same time. Students in search of a blue-riband credential are therefore taught by people who see themselves as being in the business not of 'training' administrators but of discharging the central task of Waterend: creating new knowledge.

There are at least two professors in the School of Education at Waterend who have an elegant model of the creation and transmission of such knowledge. There must be many more elsewhere. The knowledge is created by them – and in believing precisely that they are more than justified by the evidence. It is then propagated through their students (the best of whom will teach elsewhere), through their own books, and, most widely of all, through second-order text books which are then generally used for the education and training of practitioners.

This explication of a model is admittedly an over-simplification; but there is no sense in which it is meant to be a parody. For the moment, it leaves unexplained and unexamined the process by which the nature and content of what is researchable and worthy of research are defined in the first place. What is striking about it is the hierarchical view of dissemination, as well as the apparent distancing of the 'real' world of practitioners or even of students who are to be educated/trained as practitioners. At one level, the model reads like the application of an 'arts and sciences' model to the working of a professional school. In a later section of this book, we return to this theme and to the contrasts with other professional schools that arise because of the application.

Above all, and most immediately for this thumb-nail sketch of Waterend, the model throws into sharp relief the scholar-practitioner and faculty-student relationships there. In the Waterend School of Education, the problem is at once simplified and complicated by the absence of students engaged in courses of teacher preparation. This is one of the schools (few in number but powerful in influence and example) that have chosen to play no part in preparing entrants to the teaching profession. It would be a fundamental error to suppose that simply because the school is exotic it has no influence.

Long before the time of Dean Strong, the university had resolved, without controversy, not to become involved in undergraduate teacher education. That was properly the business of the big state schools. But there had developed a strong and (in terms of recruitment) magnetic degree course called the 'Master of Arts in Teaching' (MAT). The course attracted graduates from other universities, and more colleges, who came to Waterend's School of Education for two years, there to imbibe a heady blend of courses in their specialities. To the college graduates, the leading scholars of the School of Education made little or no contribution, although their research assistants did and enjoyed the emoluments, as well as, sometimes, the work. But this sector of the School, organized for the most part as a separate unit, was dominated by specialists in 'curriculum and instruction'. Many of these specialists specialised in mathematics education or teaching in the social sciences. The books they wrote, when they wrote any, were clearly different from those explicitly aimed at creating the kind of new knowledge a hard-nosed social scientist would respect.

Dean Strong anticipated the day when the market for the MAT might begin to sag. Meanwhile, he found the whole enterprise, if not embarrassing, at least out of tune with his overarching objective of dedicating the School to the study of education. Whatever else the MAT was, and whatever its value and appeal, it represented something a good deal messier than that. As a skilful man of principle, Dean Strong obeyed the commandment not to kill and sheltered in the concession that he need not strive officiously to keep the MAT alive.

For a variety of reasons, MAT enrolments began to decline gradually, and the valves controlling the inflow of outside money began to close. Soon the flow might be only a trickle. Applications from minority groups declined more sharply as their members found progressively easier access to other, admittedly more prestigious, professions. Decline accelerated, hastened by the routine operations of established committee procedures. The academic standards of the Waterend School of Education were, in any case, being sharpened. As each appointment in curriculum and instruction came up for review, whether for tenure or for advancement, it became clearer that, on stated and objective criteria, the applicants must be at a severe disadvantage. They had not published at all or had not published enough or had published in the wrong places. Their associated departments — mathematics, history — did not fight for them. In a few years they had all gone, and the MAT was dead.

Few regarded the demise of the MAT as much more than a mild misfortune. Among those few, however, were some of the most spirited teachers in a secondary school adjoining the campus. With its extensive programme of internships, the MAT had, for that school at least, kept open links with a neighbour properly regarded as a leading influence in educational thought and development. The links may have been slight, but they were there, and they served as a kind of pledge of commitment to the work of elementary and secondary schools. Without such links there would not have developed the involvement of the faculty in an experimental school. However distant and inappropriate the analogies, here was something which at least began to approach the concern of Waterend's medical school with the formation of practitioners and the promotion of medical science. In the case of the MAT — but not necessarily because of it — that all died.

In the few weeks before his retirement, Dean Strong read two newspaper articles. One article was an account of an acrimonious dispute in a neighbouring state over control of the licencing procedure for teachers. Representatives of the teachers' associations argued that all universities, and pre-eminently those that beat the drum for the rest, had retreated further into their ivory towers. They knew little, and cared less, about teachers in schools. They might still have institutional control over teacher education, but control over the licencing of teachers (and therefore, in the long run, over the courses that contribute to that process) would be wrested from them.

The other article described Strong's own university's business school, across the bay in an imposing sky-scraper. At the centre of its effort lay the M.B.A. programme. The programme rewarded teaching as well as research, or so the reporter believed; and the existence of the two tenure tracks was freely recognised. Each year 40,000 students enquired about admission; 6,700 applied, although completion of the application form was known to consume about forty hours. Of these, 970 were accepted and 790 presented themselves. At the end of their two-year course, the number of offers of employment made through the School exceeded the number of graduates.

Dean Strong wondered about the place of his own school in the family of graduate schools, and about its relationship to the world of public schools it was originally created to serve. For a few years after retirement, he accepted a part-time visiting appointment at Highside University, where he had served some of his own apprenticeship in the professoriate.

CHAPTER III

Highside

Highside State University (HSU on the T-shirts and nearly everywhere else) plays football very well but keeps it in its place. Indeed, the university is, as far as possible, determined either to do a thing well or not to do it at all. Several of its graduate professional schools appear, with cheerful regularity, well up on the list of national ratings. The president is glad that education is now among them. HSU was a land-grant institution, its policies and governance well tuned (after long practice) to the needs of the community and to the policies and prejudices of the legislature. If it ever tried to climb into an ivory tower, it would certainly look silly, and would probably fall out.

Its graduate school of education (to employ the preferred title, which appears on the school's letterhead but is hardly a complete description) has not always been in its present position, least of all in the eyes of the administration. Older members of the faculty are fond of recalling the occasion when the provost addressed them at a special meeting. His message was clear, only partly welcome, and (they thought) hardly warranted by the facts. In brief, he told them that education was at the bottom of the totem pole, and it was up to them to do something about it, and fast.

The delivery of this message more or less coincided with the arrival of Dean Tough — as distinguished in his own field, sociology, as the provost was in biochemistry. New appointments were created, a handful of stars translated from the constellations of Waterend and elsewhere. Again, as has so often been the case, the system of tenure and promotion was used to give effect to a desired institutional improvement. At this particular university, decisions on such matters were taken by a central universitywide committee (known locally, and for obscure reasons, as 'the Steer') which, in each case, appointed an *ad hoc* committee of experts. In dealing with the School of Education, the Steer showed none of the tenderness it had often displayed towards law, medicine, and even business.

Certainly the Steer was unwilling to rubber-stamp decisions, having already consumed a great deal of time wrangling with Dean Tough's predecessor, and it did not hesitate to implant in the *ad hoc* committees representatives from the humanities, natural sciences, and social sciences. As the School pressed for more tenured appointments, the provost, dean and Steer amiably conspired to spell out the criteria. Again, the writing of text books and the rendering of consultancy either did not 'count' or were thought not to count (which, in the end, came to the same thing), or they did not count as much as research and publications as defined in terms the Steer was sympathetic with.

More publication meant more visibility and higher national repute. The provost and the president beamed as the School nudged up the tables. Research funds were attracted and credit was reflected upon HSU as a whole.

Subtle institutional changes began to take place within the School, which conferred the Ed.D. and not the Ph.D. (jealously guarded by Arts and Sciences). HSU established a graduate college, admission to which was coveted even by the most securely established faculty. Only members of the Graduate College can compose a committee for a doctoral degree, and not more than half the more senior members of the School of Education have been admitted to the College. At least one adviser, secure in reputation and within months of retirement, resigned in protest from the Graduate College after another long wrangle over the subject and methodology of a proposed thesis. With the adviser's support, the proposal was for work (in which the candidate had been personally involved) on the resolution of desegregation difficulties in a city nearby. The committee, tuned to the values of the Graduate College, disliked it as being too close to current controversy, likely to be lacking in objectivity, and not based upon any generally accepted methodology.

Parallel to these changes, which powerfully mirror a change in the underlying values of a school, were other institutional subtleties. Although, in much public parlance, *school* and *graduate school* are interchangeable, with the unspoken assumption that the latter is superior to the former, only faculty who are members of the Graduate College are now listed as members of the Graduate School. Admission to the College is not, of course, controlled within the School. Similarly, there was created a puzzling distinction between *school* and *department*. *School* became the more comprehensive term, embracing the department (which had its own chairman) as well as the various institutes that sprang up around it. Only members of the senate count as members of the department, the core of the activity of which is defined as research. Many externally funded projects found a home in the institutes which, in turn, provided much-needed employment and support for graduate students. The details matter only as a partial illustration of the way in which the more or less immutable laws of the labour market and the (often apparently trivial) niceties of constitutional and administrative details can combine to propel an institution in a particular direction. In this case, although the gap remains wide and permanent, the direction was undoubtedly towards at least some of the ruling ideals of Waterend.

Dean Tough, an intellectual and a realist, gave more than ten of the best years of his life to building the School on a well-defined foundation. He realised that not everything could be done well and therefore should not be attempted. 'Either well or not at all' was a slogan he too understood. Moreover, he knew that HSU respected the 'hardness' of science more than the speculative 'softness' of the humanities, that the local world of which it was a central part was hospitable to technology and not unsympathetic to the values of technocracy.

Within seven years of his arrival, and of the provost's now almost legendary intervention, sixty of the one hundred and thirty faculty in the School of Education were psychologists. HSU was, in a cluster of related fields, noted and in a big way. Research funds were tapped to support the institutes. Special Education, Reading, and Evaluation have become — at the level of graduate work — the brightest jewels in the School's crown.

What, in all this, of the students? For some, the reviving school at Highside offers incomparable opportunities. Those able graduates who, in psychology or elsewhere, found interests that matched their own might work their way to research assistantships. Even for them, though, contracting opportunities and funding often present problems. Their graduate education might prove to be too narrow, with their employment or promotion prospects correspondingly attenuated. On the whole, however, their lot was, and is, a favoured one.

At HSU, such graduate students seem never to have constituted more than a minority. At other, by no means undistinguished, schools of education students with lives like theirs hardly exist. On a larger scale the work of survey and analysis has yet to be undertaken, but at HSU something is known of the typical graduate student in education; that student turns out to be significantly different from the student in most other professional schools. The psychology specialist, that most favoured character among HSU education students, perversely turns out to be not unlike many good graduate students in the (nonprofessional) Department of Psychology. He or she might even have *preferred* to be there.

I say *she* because the typical graduate student in Education at HSU is more likely to be a woman than a man. She is older (by as much as ten years) than students in law or medicine. She tends to have a lower G.R.E. score. Although most, perhaps nearly all, graduate students at HSU work a good part of every week and for most of the year during which they pursue advanced degrees, the education student is under much greater pressure than most others. This student tends to keep the full-time job, or a preferred successor to it, that was held before the student went back to school. In terms of its demands, and often its location some distance from the campus, that job tends to be strenuous, both personally and professionally. That is why (and here, HSU is not unique) so many courses are given late in the day. The assistant headmaster of a secondary school, travelling twenty miles at the end of a day not likely to have been relaxed, should thus not be compared with the (probably younger) law student who undertakes some fifteen hours of part-time work near or even on campus.

The graduate student in education is, if he or she is already working in classrooms, likely to be pursuing a qualification that, with luck, will enable him or her to move away from the classroom or from school altogether. This student is just as likely to be making his or her way purposefully up what was once the wide ladder of 'higher education administration', another central specialty of HSU. Until 1979 there was a residency requirement; no student could move beyond a certain point in advancing through doctoral studies without spending at least one year in full-time study. Declining enrolments and rising costs swept that requirement away.

So much for the graduates. Even at HSU, justly proud of its place among the finest graduate schools of education, most students in education are, in fact, undergraduates. Here, the numbers may be deceptive. For a graduate to be a student in education means — in terms of campus activity at least — to be a full-time student in that field and nowhere else. An undergraduate, on the other hand, may, at different stages of a standard four-year career leading to the baccalaureate, devote to education anywhere from a fragment of his or her time to a large part of it.

At HSU, the School of Education is a place to which the undergraduate student goes from a base in arts and sciences or from which the student issues (if majoring in elementary education) in pursuit of suitable complements to the overall course in education. The distribution requirements — the rubric that prescribes the courses the undergraduate may, or must, take and in what combination — are admirably flexible. In that respect, the undergraduate is unlike his or her exact contemporary who is bound for engineering and for whom the regulations are (and, everybody assumes, must be) much more precise. It is possible — almost — to qualify as a teacher and certainly possible to take numerous courses in education in a prolonged fit of absentmindedness.

At Highside, in spite of the pride of the School of Education, admission standards to courses in education are not high in terms of the required grade point average. Dean Tough has never been happy about this. Taking proper advantage of the fact that the national demand for teachers was on the decline, two years ago he took firm but careful steps to elevate the requirements. His own school, accepting the possibility that this could lead to a further drop in enrolment, nevertheless supported him. As it turned out, the proposal was defeated by a group of deans and professors from the natural sciences who, with the honesty that sometimes springs from apprehension or anger, successfully objected on one ground alone: they asserted that if Education were to do such a thing, they would be deprived of what one of them inelegantly described as 'our dumping ground'.

Dean Tough did not repeat his attempt. His colleagues related the failure to an even bolder initiative taken some four years earlier. On that occasion a small group of leaders of opinion in the School of Education, uneasy about their hermaphroditic status in a world of graduate and undergraduate categories, promoted the recommendation that undergraduate teacher education be abandoned. After all, there were plenty of other places in the state where the appropriate courses could be taken and the requirements of licencing satisfied.

On this occasion, as on the more recent one, opposition came from outside rather than inside the School of Education. The key to that opposition was the fear that, should such a purifying measure be effective, HSU would lose many students, some of them very good students. Why should they spend four years, even at HSU, and not collect (in case they should need it) a teacher's licence when they could do precisely that elsewhere? Alternatively, why should the sons and daughters of tax-paying citizens — who might want to become teachers with no unconventional extra investment of money — be deprived of the privilege of attending the flagship campus?

The president's office reinforced these doubts by pointing out that the university could make itself most unpopular with the legislature by retreating from its public commitment to provide teachers for the schools, as well as to provide lawyers, agriculturalists, civil servants, dentists, and other categories. After all, this was a land-grant university.

So, it seems, undergraduate teacher education is here to stay at Highside, but perhaps on a reduced scale. It seems, too, that the magnetism of the graduate school distorts policy and priorities. From time to time, the dean and his associates make brave public efforts to reconcile, both in their own minds and on the official agenda, the style and objectives of the graduate and undergraduate enterprises. One formula has been to stress that the School's commitment is to research ('the *study* of education') and that it must be concerned *inter alia* with research in teacher education. Indeed, its distinctive contribution to that large and inchoate field is precisely to *study* it rather than to *work* in it. This policy has resulted, from time to time, in units, laboratories, and institutes for the study of teacher education being created or abolished. Nobody is claiming they have made much difference.

One undergraduate in his senior year has provided a serviceable account of how his academic time is divided up. He takes courses each week in arts and sciences, in this case, history, English and social studies. These are taught, of course, with no special reference to the needs of teachers. Indeed, there's no reason why they should be. Over the past two years, this undergraduate has taken a series of courses in 'foundations' in the School of Education. The School has distinguished scholars in psychology and sociology (and much else besides), but their time and attention are pre-empted by graduate work and their own research. The courses are therefore taught by assistants, some very good and some not, who are graduate students earning the money (or exemption from tuition fees) necessary to pursue their doctorates. Without the availability of such work, many graduate students would not be able to support themselves.

So much for the first two elements in this undergraduate's course work. He also needs instruction in the methodology of English teaching; for this, he goes to the School of Education and not the English Department (which would not be the case if some other subject were one of his main fields). Here, he meets a professor of curriculum and instruction, the author of several profitable text books, who describes himself as a 'reflective practitioner'. Inevitably, it has been some years since this professor taught in schools and, indeed, some years since the latest in a series of short-lived and half-hearted attempts to create 'clinical professors' was abandoned. He is not a member of the Graduate College but occasionally takes a modest part in supervising graduate work. He is surprised whenever a pilgrim to the campus and the School seeks him out. The 'action', he has come to believe, is elsewhere.

As part of his course work over the last two years, the student, in his senior year, completed several weeks of student teaching (practice teaching) in local schools. His work was supervised by a co-ordinator designated by the university and recognized as an effective teacher of English language and literature. It is the task of the co-ordinator to guide the student through the shoals and rapids of class-room teaching. The student, being reflective and well motivated, cannot yet see (and wonders if he ever will) whether and how the four fragments of learning and experience — subject-matter subjects, foundations, work in curriculum and instruction, and student teaching — will be related anywhere else than in the School's catalogue. His coordinator cares about him but doesn't work for nothing. The coordinator's reward is a number of tuition units which he cashes in on campus as a substantial contribution to his course. He is well on his way towards his doctorate in, of course, the Graduate School of Education and hopes one day soon to become a director of curriculum at a good suburban school.

CHAPTER IV

The Market and the Monastery

What general observations, if any, may be derived from contemplation of these two hypothetical case-studies, Waterend and Highside? For me they serve, above all, as a warning against easy transatlantic gener-alisations. I believe that schools and departments of education throughout the world experience acute difficulty in locating them-selves properly in their academic and professional spheres. But the special case of the graduate school in the United States ought not simply to be allowed to lie under the umbrella of that all-embracing, and therefore not very useful, remark. Americans take less kindly than Europeans to the notion that, to some problems, there exist no satisfac-tory solutions.

I was therefore impressed but not surprised by the frequency with which enquiries were made in the course of my travels and talks about the possibilities of 'changing' or 'improving' the status of graduate schools of education in research universities or of all schools of educa-tion in all universities (for I wish to argue later that the issues are indissolubly linked). The underlying, widely prevalent assumptions are that something is wrong and that something can and should be done about it. These assumptions are made and expressed just as often by people outside as by those inside schools of education — although, in the former case, with more vehemence and in the latter, with greater understanding.

Are such assumptions justified? I ask this question for several good reasons. It seems unfortunate that the canard 'schools of education are at the bottom of the pile and deserve to be' should be repeated so often with no serious attempt to discover precisely what the canard means. It is no great fun to work in places that are constantly sniffed at or spat upon. Moreover, the implication that the schools themselves are somehow 'at fault' carries with it the suggestion that dramatic and relevant improvements can be made, within and by those very same institutions.

I should prefer to approach the question from the other end, with the privileges of an observer standing outside the system. It may be that, in consequence, what follows is somewhat determinist or even defeatist in tone, for what I want to stress, and at some length, is that the G.S.E.'s (an abbreviation for 'graduate school of education', to be used hereafter) are indeed firmly trapped within their appointed place in a complicated world. Although they may wriggle about inside that space, it is unreasonable to suppose that they could, collectively or individually, leap into a new and better position by an exercise of superhuman will or supreme intelligence.

The generalisation I now wish to test is that the puzzle about American G.S.E.'s is, in very large measure, explained by the fact that they operate within the laws of the market, laws which they may themselves influence at the margins but which they cannot fundamentally change. If the British university behaves like a monastery, the American university operates as and within a market.

That metaphored comparison is meant to be insulting or flattering to neither party, although, if I were obliged to choose, I should have to express some preference for the open market over the cloistered monastery. What characteristics of the universities I know best in Britain do I have in mind in presuming to describe them as 'monastic'?

Not, certainly such engaging qualities as antiquity, celibacy, ceremony, irrelevance to or isolation from the real world — although a half-serious case could be made for each of these. More important points need to be made, however, if the contrast with the 'market' is to be a real one. British universities are designed for a carefully nurtured minority, and entry to them is by a rigidly applied test of academic suitability. They are not very numerous and, although these things aren't absolute, within the charmed number of forty-five, relatively clear orders of reputation and achievement are nationally recognised. Even more important, the number of universities is in effect defined by central government, which has created 'alongside them' (nobody must ever say or even think *'beneath* them') other institutions of higher education called 'polytechnics'. Polytechnics are expected to be more applied, less theoretical, less dedicated to the cultivation of fundamental research. They do not, to their unconcealed chagrin, confer their own degrees and their students tend to be, in conventional terms, less well qualified than their university counterparts.

The British university receives from the national government a block grant, which is assessed in order to take account of the number of students — a relatively stable commodity, given that provision is made only for a minority of the relevant age group. The undergraduate student who has won a place at a university receives an allowance of cash amounting to a salary, and all fees ('tuition') are paid. The undergraduate chooses to study the subject found most attractive, in which the student takes the greatest intellectual or personal pleasure, and such half-hearted attempts as have been made to introduce manpower-planning have collapsed in disrepute. Most bachelors move straight into employment, without undue difficulty and without further formal education. They will have spent some three years as full-time students, and transfer of any kind from one university to another is extremely rare.

Only a few become graduate students, and those few that do so become research students in the classical arts and sciences sense. Part-time students (except, significantly, in education) are rare, as are mature students. Most graduate research students receive full grants from government agencies. Very few of them take, or could take, paid employment.

So much for the British university and its typical student. The applicability of the monastery metaphor is, I hope, by now sufficiently obvious. The undergraduate student is one of a small and carefully recruited elite. This student, we assume, has an academic vocation. That will be tested, in the subject of his or her choosing, by the pursuit, for three uninterrupted years, of a rigorous and specialised course. The student may not interrupt the course nor take parts of it in different places; he or she is *enclosed*. The university where the student resides is protected from the necessity of making an income by receiving grants, the distribution of which pays little or no attention to any wordly success of the university. The university lives on alms, endowments, and a guaranteed public gift.[1] The student is fully supported by and through that university for as long as he or she remains a member of it. The undergraduate is unlikely to become a graduate student except in medicine, which is always and everywhere different. If the student qualifies for 'research', he or she may expect the levels of

---

[1] There is no intended irony in these sentences, although I am only too well aware, as these pages are written, of the pressure now being brought to bear upon university finances by the economic recession and the policies of the U.K. government. Universities are no longer 'protected' in the sense that they need not worry unduly about their revenues. Nevertheless, with marginal exceptions, they do not seek funds elsewhere than from government. Nor is there (as of early 1982) a suggestion that any foreseeable government proposes to introduce new criteria for the distribution of resources to universities. They may shrink, and parts of them may shrivel; but they are not in the market place.

enclosure, commitment, and support to at least be maintained. Most students, after their three-year undergraduate novitiate, move into relatively superior employment. Law is an undergraduate study, but vocational preparation for the profession is undertaken outside the university.

To define the monastery as small, enclosed, residential, protected, securely endowed, assuring secular salvation is, by contrast, to describe the market and return to the G.S.E.'s. American students do not expect full public support and would not accept the restrictions, either in numbers or the pattern of studies, that go with it. They expect to make their own way, with varying measures of support — some public, perhaps, as well as family and personal — through a complex system of undergraduate and graduate studies. They are obliged to spend real money, and they expect eventually to see financial returns. For similar reasons, universities — public or private, large or small, famous or obscure — need to do those things and to be perceived as doing them well, which will attract support, research funds, and — always the bottom line — tuition-paying students who expect a return on an investment of time, opportunity, and money. They need to offer a flexible range of courses, graduate and undergraduate, to bring in good and honest business.

I, therefore, ask the reader, whether English or American, in reading the following pages to keep in mind the features of Waterend and Highside as he now perceives them. I also ask the reader to remember that those pages have been written about a market by a vagrant monk who promised to write an 'essay'.

Undergraduates

The trouble with G.S.E.'s is that inevitably they have something to do with teachers, even if that something often means as little as possible. And the trouble with teachers is that they are painfully undervalued — everywhere, perhaps, but especially in the United States. I cannot count the number of times this point was made to me, but often obliquely, as though it had little or nothing to do with the discomfort of G.S.E.'s. It is precisely here that the contrast with lawyers and law schools becomes most pronounced. Law schools surely derive much of their prestige and success from the importance and prosperity of the lawyer in American life. The social and economic status of the lawyer has steadily advanced in recent decades. Smart people are thus ready to go to law schools, and smarter people to teach in them.

Not only teacher-politicians but detached observers of the scene comment wryly that teachers get only eighty percent of the pay of garbage collectors. Since, in any case, it is possible to qualify as a teacher wholly within an undergraduate course, it is hardly surprising that recruitment to G.S.E.'s is problematic. Yet G.S.E.'s remain closely linked to teachers and ex-teachers and their careers. I do not pretend to understand why (in terms other than those exclusively economic) the image of the teacher in the United States is so tarnished. To be sure, the job isn't overwhelmingly attractive elsewhere either; but it is clear that in a society which places so high an explicit value on education and schooling, there must be complicating factors.

Some of these factors can be identified in broad terms and without undue difficulty. The democratic style of American life and therefore of American schools exposes the ordinary teacher to the kind of commentary and criticism, by pupils and adults alike, against which teachers in more static or stagnant societies are usually protected. Public doubt about the effectiveness of schooling, in the propagation of which some G.S.E.'s have played no small part, reflects no credit on teachers and erodes their self-esteem. Neither the radical nor the liberal Left nor the conservative back-to-basics Right is perceived as encouraging the idea that schooling is succeeding (whatever that may mean) and that teachers deserve credit, in all its many forms.

Moreover, it may be a misleading oversimplification to argue that Americans place a particularly high value on 'education' in some broad and unspecific sense, starting from induction into a liberal, humane culture. Many Americans have themselves commented on the national tendency to value education for what it can deliver, for the credentials it can furnish, for the gates to prosperity and status it opens. To say so much is to draw attention to the dark side of the meritocracy or the belief in mobility. Emphasis upon such desirable principles leads to undervaluing the forms of education not viewed as instrumental. Such emphasis also tends to diminish the dignity of teaching as perceived (although it would be wrong to exaggerate this contrast) in more traditional or static societies.

At a time of unprecedented economic difficulty, taxes for the support of schools are among the relatively few items of public expenditure that can be, with relative constitutional ease, attacked through propaganda or the ballot box. What's more, teachers in the United States have long (perhaps always) been severely limited in the exercise of anything that might be considered professional autonomy. School boards, directly and through appointed superintendents, expect to resolve all important questions related to educational policy and practice. Teachers are made to feel that they are no more than the hired servants of volatile bodies for which they often have little respect. Teachers have no clients; they only have patrons.

Problems have been multiplied, so many local critics allege, by deliberate, high-minded attempts to use the school to effect massive social reforms. Desegregation measures, for example, inevitably have made many schools, especially those traditionally the preserve of a white middle class, much less agreeable, even threatening places in which to work. This may be saying no more than that teachers in many such schools now have much more difficult tasks (as well, doubtless, as much more worth-while) than those of their predecessors. It shouldn't be surprising, then, if many ordinary, intelligent people prefer a less exposed and better-paying job. Anyone can be idealistic at the expense of somebody else.

More than once, I was told that one effect of the substitution of social for narrow educational (or pedagogic) goals has been to discourage from going into elementary schools — or still more clearly — into secondary schools many teachers who otherwise would have gone into those schools. That may be so, but it certainly must be the case that many of those who in other, more restricted societies choose a career in school-teaching (*faute de mieux*, it may often be), in the United

States prefer to teach or work in some area of higher education. That would hardly be surprising, even if the financial rewards were no greater, and it serves as an illustration of the operation of the marketplace principle. Higher education in the United States produces myriad students but at the same time consumes a good proportion of them as well.

For such reasons as these, teaching in schools is not attractive to many able young people with a wide choice of careers, and it could be that it is becoming even less attractive. The consequences for G.S.E.'s are at once obvious and profound. In the real world which they, along with the rest of us, are obliged to inhabit, they cannot define themselves as being in the business of making teachers. That is largely an undergraduate business and, for reasons over which a school or university has no control whatever, is largely an unattractive one. Because the job is not attractive, they are required (as will appear) to distance themselves from it in other ways. It is from the ranks of that unjustly undervalued profession, however, that many of their own graduate students will come, with a variety of purposes and ambitions. For the most part, those students will not wish to remain as teachers even if they became teachers in the first place.

That is the contradiction that lies at the heart of the G.S.E., a contradiction that led one distinguished faculty member in one noted G.S.E. to express his opinion of, and defend his pleasure at not having to work with, 'dumb-assed teachers'. It is a contradiction that isn't their fault, of course, but still one that is singularly difficult to live comfortably with. One technique of resolving part of this contradiction is to make a distinction between researchers and managers (which is what the G.S.E. is all about) and rank-and-file teachers (who are not of their world). In this technique, the analogy of the business school is often deployed at this point. Such schools are not concerned with shop-floor workers, nor yet with secretaries, but with managers grown in a different soil. But that's just it: in education almost all the managers and many of the researchers are drawn from the ranks of those who have once been, however briefly, 'teachers'.

More illuminating in many ways is the contrast with the market of the law school, that mirage of esteem, scholarship and power, dancing on the horizon for deans Strong and Tough. Such schools are not, I was assured, without their problems. They, too, must reconcile the tensions of the academic-professional dualism. Practitioners criticise them for being too theoretical and academic purists for concerning themselves with the mechanical trivia and routine of a lawyer's office.

The market and traditions of an ancient profession sustain them. Able men and women (the latter in increasing numbers, at least at Waterend) come to such schools with excellent records to pursue demanding three-year courses immediately after winning their bachelor's degrees. Others, also in a growing proportion, come with several years of experience and employment and invest their savings in a Juris Doctor degree. All are assured of excellent prospects as lawyers, in an enlarging variety of careers and specialised fields. A few years ago, many of them would have pursued a Ph.D. or an academic career; they have turned from that to law, not to teaching. It's not difficult to see why.

Of course, Waterend is not the world, nor does it want to be. Other places require less — less tuition, less commitment, easier packages of full-time and part-time study, lower standards of admission and achievement, more modest expectations. That precisely is the charm of the market, when it works well. A J.D. from Waterend can expect to 'do better' than most others: he knows what he is buying with his ability, time, and money. For a G.S.E. to flourish in this kind of world and on these terms certainly won't be easy. As though that in itself weren't difficult enough, they face another severe disadvantage. Almost though not quite universally, and unlike any other major graduate professional school, the work and reputation of a G.S.E. is interwoven with what happens in undergraduate teacher education and training.

What strikes a visitor from Europe is the remarkable variety of institutions and patterns within which such undergraduate teacher education takes place. It is possible to become a teacher in the United States by following programmes in a large number of fairly small liberal arts colleges, with no strong or overriding commitment to this particular task. Many more intending or possible teachers follow structurally similar programmes in schools or departments of education within larger universities. In many of these universities there are no strong graduate programmes in education: the main burden of work is at undergraduate level.

Within a smaller number of well-known universities there have, of course, developed schools of education which strongly emphasise graduate level work while inevitably preserving, as at Highside, a heavy but not always proud involvement in undergraduate teacher education. Only a tiny number have, like Waterend, severed altogether the undergraduate connection.

This is why I argue that perceptions of the nature and quality of

G.S.E.'s are interwoven with what happens in the mainstream of teacher education and training and, indeed, with perceptions of school teaching itself. Students in G.S.E.'s are or have been teachers. G.S.E.'s belong to a straggling family of institutions in which undergraduate students are trained as teachers.

In what, then, does that undergraduate study of education consist? This is an important question even for those schools (very few, in any case) that have managed to abandon such study. The reputation of education is in all places, but especially, of course, where the undergraduate element is present, entangled with views on and recollections of what happens and what does not happen at the lower level. In particular, the representatives of the heartland of arts and sciences have never quite reconciled themselves to what happens over the road or around the corner in education.

Nor would it be easy for them to do so, given the behaviour of the market on the one hand (few of them could, in present circumstances, 'do without' the presence of a school of education), and, on the other, the unsatisfactorily haphazard way in which present arrangements have developed over time. The example of Highside well illustrates this truth. It is hard to shake the conviction — based on expediency rather than careful argument, as it doubtless is — that teachers can be trained and educated within the general context and constraints of an undergraduate career. Only a decent minimum of concessions to specialised or professional requirements need be made. That is true of training for and access to no other profession, certainly to none on the scale of education.

The explanation of this odd state of affairs is, for the most part, historical. In the American tradition, as in certain strands of its European counterpart, a 'liberal education' has long been perceived as part of the necessary equipment of a self-respecting teacher. The frontiers of definition between a subject as 'part of a liberal education' (history, for example) and the same study as 'the content of what the teacher will teach' are imprecise and changeable. Indeed, many of the great universities of the United States had their origins in normal schools or in a legislative requirement that they produce a sufficient supply of teachers and other public servants. Moreover, the more open and flexible structure of American undergraduate courses — where English forms of specialisation do not flourish — make this identification of the higher education of teachers with the acquisition of the content of their later teaching at once more plausible and more defensible.

It has, on the other hand, made it singularly difficult to develop a general, coherent view of what the education of the teacher *per se* should be, or to develop a sensible distinction between academic and professional elements in the teacher's course. Indeed, the most sustained, recent enterprise to offer such a coherent interpretation has led its author into a lengthy criticism of almost every necessary part of the present system. In 'A Design for a School of Pedagogy' (1980), Bunnie Smith systematically analyses the weaknesses in the present system: dispersed over too many institutions of dubious quality, confused with undergraduate studies, lacking both academic rigour and professional relevance. Smith concludes, with some marginal reservations on pre-professional studies, that the exercise he deliberately calls 'pedagogy', rather than the cloudy 'education', should be confined to graduates pursuing a two-year course with a strong clinical base. His arguments for the separation of teacher training from undergraduate work are incontrovertible and are likely to have a profound influence on future development. But not all his readers, however willing in principle, will be able to accept the full majesty of his claim that a science of pedagogy already exists and that all we must do is apply it.

Present arrangements for undergraduate teacher education — upon which the schools of education, taken as a whole, necessarily depend — turn out to be indefensible. At least, they seem to have no defenders. Nobody, in the course of my long series of conversations, has yet expressed the opinion that the arrangements at Highside merit serious discussion or defence. The whole enterprise, therefore, rests upon a deeply institutionalised error. The fragments of teacher education are not related because they cannot be. Teaching by 'subject-matter' departments proceeds well or ill according to the prevailing standard of the department or its parent university or to the vagaries of external events. Student teaching, or practice teaching, is required, but, for the most part, it appears to be held at arm's length by the university. Certainly there is none of the intimacy of involvement that characterises medical education. For the most part, courses in the undergirding disciplines of education (psychology, sociology, and the philosophy and history of education) still proceed in a third compartment; courses in methods of teaching school subjects are in the fourth compartment.

This unloved system is sustained by market forces, as I have attempted to define them. The men and women of arts and sciences make no pretence of loving what they see. Many believe that time spent in a school or college of education is time wasted. Few would have done anything of the sort themselves (for were they not determined to become teachers in *higher* education?) and will not encourage their brighter students in that direction. But the school of education does have its uses. It can absorb a goodly number of weaker students, and it has had sufficient practice in such absorption. What is more, the excision of courses in education from the undergraduate curriculum would weaken the university and drive away prospective students. In a public university, moreover, it would weaken the case for favourable treatment by public authority (state and federal governments). Even if that argument could be won, the university would still need, as was discovered at Highside, to attract students by competing against other excellent institutions without offering the bonus of a teacher's license. Anyway, why should anyone pay extra in order to be paid less than a garbage collector?

Moreover, the strength of the G.S.E. depends in numerous ways on the existence of undergraduate work in education. Without that foundation, much of graduate work in education would simply have no basis. The number of students would slump, and the range of courses provided would be too narrow. Undergraduate courses may not be taught by professors and assistant professors; but that is precisely the point. In the subtle working of the academic labour market, such courses provide work and finance for teaching assistants who, in most cases, are undertaking advanced work in graduate schools of education. Thus, neither arts and sciences nor the leading figures in the G.S.E.'s have great respect for much of the work in education in their own universities. Neither group, however, could easily dispense with it, except perhaps in unusually strong and confident universities. Meanwhile, those leading figures in American graduate schools of education hope that attention will shift to graduate work and to the ways in which graduate schools establish themselves in a hard world. And so it must.

CHAPTER VI

Graduates

Graduate schools of education, like any other part of the market, need to recruit both students and faculty. For a graduate professional school, success consists in attracting very good people in both categories and in matching the needs or expectations of one group to the knowledge and skills of the other. Such simple truths help explain why G.S.E.'s seem to have so difficult a time.

In the first place, students at G.S.E.'s are unlike those of any other graduate school. On many campuses, the feeling I detected outside the G.S.E. is that some odd animals (not necessarily dangerous or offensive) were being let into the zoo. They tend to be older than most graduate students, and more of them are women or belong to minority groups. An unusually high proportion not only have full-time jobs but unusually demanding jobs. These students, quite understandably, tend to take longer to fulfil their course requirements, and they present more special cases for consideration. More of them than in any other graduate school are taking courses for specific, limited professional reasons: to acquire a new credential, secure the renewal or extension of a teacher's licence, advance a step or more along a salary scale. Their scores in the Graduate Record Examination are lower than those secured or required for entry to other graduate schools. Even friendly critics find most such students intellectually timorous, all too often justifying their place at or near the bottom of the academic heap. It's only too easy for other departments to quip that G.S.E.'s, even some good ones, will take any bodies, provided they're warm. Nor is it easy to discover, in some of the less demanding master's programmes, for example, just what margin of choice exists between the number of applicants and the number of admissions. To do any work at all, good or otherwise, a G.S.E. must remain in business.

There is another peculiarity about G.S.E.'s as a group which, as I have already hinted, carries a deep, and probably dangerous, contradiction. G.S.E.'s are not concerned with teaching; they cannot afford to be. Most of their students, certainly those at the doctoral level, are upward and outward bound from the classroom. The rich diversity of occupations in the field of education, and the importance to many career changes of a formally validated qualification, make this exodus a largely American phenomenon. There is always the possibility of employment in regional laboratories, national or state agencies, foundations, consultancy, curriculum development, industry or commerce, the media, counselling. The list goes on and on.

The number of opportunities explains — again in market terms — much of what G.S.E.'s do. It also makes perilous the business of 'comparing' institutions, directly or superficially, with their counterparts elsewhere. The G.S.E. serves as an escalator by which one climbs from the ranks of teaching to other, superior or more attractive occupations. Nowhere is this clearer than in what is loosely called 'administration', a major activity in all G.S.E.'s and the predominant activity in some. In order to become a principal, a teacher needs to improve his or her formal qualifications. A principal determined to become a superintendent is likely to pursue a doctorate. There are 104 chief education officers in England and Wales. So far as I am aware, none of them possesses a higher qualification in educational administration.

In the United States, then, a rich variety of careers flourishes in education, most such careers (like the proliferation of professional administrators in higher education) having little to do with teaching. Because such careers exist, and because access to them is, for the most part, channelled through the gates of credentialling, the keepers of those gates exact a toll. That is the way the system works. The system is not a monopoly, however. To flourish, the G.S.E. must be attractive in a highly competitive market. In particular, what must the G.S.E. do to remain at or near the top of the national league? It must, of course, have an effective sales, recruitment, and placement policy. Somewhere in the office of most deans will be found bright people (almost certainly, themselves products of G.S.E.'s) who keep careful track of *alumni,* seeking good recommendations from them and placing graduates with them. Certainly, G.S.E.'s at research universities need to operate such a network, and they do so with great skill and energy. In that respect, they do not, of course, differ from other professional schools. But in the long run, the quality of the school depends on much more than recruitment and placement. A G.S.E. will have little hard cash of its own. If it is to be academically respected across the country, it will certainly wish to attract both generous research grants and an ample supply of doctoral students. This, and all that goes with it, requires a high place in the ratings. Those ratings may be of the kind that are published ('The Top Twenty'), which everyone modestly affects to ignore, but doesn't, or they can be more subtle or informal, based upon the gossip of the inner tribe as the drums sound from New York to San Francisco.

Such a reputation is not easily acquired, nor (which is more surprising) is it speedily lost. To some extent, such renown at once reflects and reinforces the name of the parent university. Is there, in fact, a great G.S.E. in an otherwise undistinguished university? The reputation is not likely to be based on a contribution to undergraduate education; that much is already clear. Nor will it be derived from an objective study of course evaluations or a poll of student satisfaction. Rather, it will be grounded in the esteem of faculty at G.S.E.'s elsewhere, and such esteem can be won only through publications.

The faculty at Highside understood well enough what the descending provost wanted them to do. By doing good research and writing influential articles and books, a member of the faculty was, at one and the same time, tuning himself or herself in to the values of the surrounding university and advancing his or her own school. At another university (not Highside), students observed the pressures applied to the faculty by a new dean determined to change the image of his G.S.E. and improve its performance (although not *necessarily* the quality of its service to students). 'A book every four years or four articles a year' — that was the formula.

Behind such serious frivolities lies the question: What kind of book, and what sort of articles? The answer is not difficult to find; it is well illustrated in the tenure and promotion system at Highside. That system, taken for granted in the market but wondered at (with a variety of emotions) in the monastery, has about it an effective elegance in determining institutional policies and directions. At the successful G.S.E.'s, it has been deliberately and legitimately used to align the standards — but not necessarily the purposes — of those places with graduate schools in arts and sciences, especially those in the social sciences. The test of quality must be as rigorous in education as in psychology, just as in psychology it needed to be (or once had to be) as pure and as exact as it was in physics. Work that was 'softer' or messier or less well defined in the stated terms of a defined and established discipline might be 'useful', but it did not 'count'.

All this was sufficiently clear in the academic life of Waterend, and if there is much about it that is impressive, there is not a little that is disturbing. Dean Strong was undoubtedly successful in plucking scientists and scholars from other disciplines — a tactic I was once, when surrounded by deans, rash enough to caricature as 'banditry'. It does much to explain the fragmentation of G.S.E.'s — a characteristic found in all schools, though much more visible and disturbing in a few. It is a policy that encourages in those who are transplanted the belief that they — and not in some cloudy sense, 'the School' — should determine the nature of their own work. It encourages them to distance themselves from professors of education and to develop some of the characteristics of the *prima donna*.

Why, it may be asked, should G.S.E.'s require repeated infusions of blood from elsewhere? Posing this question caused one dean to enquire reflectively whether *any* original work had ever been done in education except by those who had been imported from another discipline. It seems surprising, if such a question is justified at all, that the last half-century has not seen the growth of a relatively autonomous study of education and the establishment in it of recognised scholars who were not imported to bring distinction to the field of education.

I wish to suggest (without myself being qualified to propose remedies) that this endemic debility must be related to the structural deficiencies so clearly visible in the Waterend model. It is certainly not because the people have not been clever enough. What, then, might these structural weaknesses be? They are, I believe, related to problems now to be discussed under the headings 'anchorage' and 'linkage', problems that will prove to be closely interconnected.

First, anchorage. The trouble with G.S.E.'s is that the inexorable logic of the market has obliged them, formally in the case of Waterend and informally in that of Highside, to distance themselves from the contaminating world of practice and training. They have, in intention but not always in performance, ceased to be professional schools without ever quite becoming anything else. The culture has not grown, at least not in sufficient numbers, scholars with a commitment to improving practice based upon research. In this, G.S.E.'s differ dramatically from schools of medicine, law, and business. Academic respectability has been defined in such terms as to encourage the study, in a positivist spirit, of the exact and the measurable or, in what I wish to call an imperialist spirit, of the broad and the contextual. To this phenomenon of imperialism I must briefly return after discussing what lies behind the label *linkage*.

The problem of linkage was presented to me in one of its sharpest forms in the condensed account two Waterend professors gave of their rôle in the creation of knowledge. The question raised is that of the relationship *in education* between the thinker (or researcher), on the one hand, and, on the other, administrators, politicians, educationalists, teacher-educators, and teachers. It is, in part, a problem of the research agenda. There is in medicine a subtle, complex relationship between practice, training, and research. At the centre of this relationship lies the teaching hospital, with power and status in the hands of the chairs of the clinical departments. The work of training new doctors, the treatment of patients, the dissemination to the field of the results of research, the even more rapid incorporation in training procedures of the results of research, the generation of more research, the involvement in it of theoretical scientists who work in a spirit neither of arrogance nor of undue deference to immediate utility — to none of this can I find an analogy in education.

This is not, of course, to suggest that imitation of what I take to be the medical model would, even if it could miraculously be accomplished, necessarily achieve anything. Apart from everything else that medicine is, it is both much simpler and much more prestigious than education. I do, however, repeat that whenever I contemplate the workings of G.S.E.'s and, at a contrived distance from them, the rest of the educational world, I am afflicted by a curious sense of free-floating, of rootlessness, of the separation of what should properly be parts of a whole.

Meanwhile, the upward drift (if that's what it is) of G.S.E.'s sometimes takes other forms. One of the wisest and most distinguished men in the field observed cryptically: 'It has become very unfashionable for professors of education to have anything to do with schools'. Underlying this surprising change of fashion are layers of prejudice, snobbery, disillusionment, market calculation, and — the odd man out — creative scholarship. The message in the G.S.E.'s is: *Do not prepare teachers or school personnel or educational administrators. No credit will come to us for dealing with schools, which are messy and difficult. We have tried to make them better and failed. Teachers don't want to see us, and don't believe we have anything to say to them. Moreover, the demand is falling, and we can't just go on turning out doctorates in higher education or preparing people to be superintendents. So there are new worlds in business, in the media, in museums, in the education of the aged. We all know that schooling and education are not the same thing, that they are often in conflict. Our enrolments are badly down, so let's roll back the frontiers and make education synonymous with whatever we want to do. We are a school of education — not of pedagogy or routine administration.*

Such are the temptations of what I have labelled 'imperialism', but which a more sardonic and much better-informed critic called the 'doctrine of Anything-But': anything but schools of pedagogy, he meant. Beneath it lies, of course, a much more serious and deeply impressive reorientation of scholarly thought and historical interpretation. Beyond a doubt, it is an intellectual absurdity to treat the history (or present) of education as though it turned only on legislative or narrowly institutional questions. Correctly viewed, schooling is only one among numerous vehicles of education, and probably is not the most important. The family, apprenticeship, churches, newspapers — all are woven into a rich fabric. Perhaps a distinction should be made between Education and education.

Perhaps so, but what, then, are the implications for G.S.E.'s? One implication, of course, is that to them new scholars are attracted, representing novel and seductive forms of banditry. With these scholars, however, comes a new problem. The positivist tradition already distracts the attention of schools of education from schooling and nudges them towards a social-science tradition. The tradition increases the distance between the G.S.E.'s and ordinary practice. The imperialist perspective, also rooted in strong and disciplined traditions, albeit of history or anthropology, raises one's eyes above the plane of the schools to peaks of creative speculation.

But what of the students? Will they, in the end, come in sufficient numbers and at no small cost to follow what are being redefined as courses appropriate to a new mission for the G.S.E.? Surely many will come for traditional reasons, but it remains to be seen whether the new scholars (and it would be a mistake either to overestimate their number or to underestimate their influence) can deliver, within the context of a professional school, the support and guidance such students legitimately expect.

We are now back in the market place, though perhaps in an exotic corner of it. Nevertheless, it is a good corner from which to ask a question or two about the ways in which the overall scholarly aspirations of G.S.E.'s match the needs to be met, particularly for those taking other than doctoral courses (hereafter grouped as 'Masters').

Just as all G.S.E.'s stress the *G* and have apparently no general wish to draw attention to undergraduate work, so they tend within graduate work to concentrate — in conversation and elsewhere — on the doctors. That is where rigour, continuity, and satisfaction are to be found. Even in a public university, however, the accounts must be balanced. Only rarely can that be done on the basis of doctoral programmes alone. That may be why so many universities appear to relax (to the point of total passivity) their requirements for admission to a master's programme. Many who spoke to me seemed profoundly disturbed at the consequences of such a policy. It appears, to them at least, that holders of Master's get a raw deal. Their courses are often fragmented and under-staffed, with the result that even the most conscientious professor sags under the weight of largely repetitive work. In some places, little proof of work is needed; no attempt is made to impose a coherent pattern upon it. Many of those taking courses, or parts of them, are fulfilling requirements of employment or promotion, and their motivation is low.

The presence of these students is an uneasy counterpoint to the scholarship of social scientists and imperialists and is a further illustration of the pervasive contradiction that lies coldly at the heart of graduate schools of education. Yet in private, tuition-driven schools, their dollars are needed and in public schools 'the bottom line is always the number of enrolments'. They do not exist on the same scale in other disciplines or professions, and they cloud even the most glittering reputations.

One long-established, sensitive scholar, now migrated from a G.S.E. back to the parent department from which the bandits once took him, spoke of the problem with a mixture of anger and pain. 'Schools of education live by fraud', he concluded. He cannot have been right; but even if he were, the fault would lie at nobody's door. We are back to the structures in which, it seems, the schools are themselves embedded.

The puzzle from which this book originated is not solved and perhaps never can be. But perhaps now its intractable nature is more sharply defined. It turns out to be not so very surprising that a nation which values education so highly should pay such scant regard to its graduate schools of education. The hypothetical case-studies of Waterend and Highside serve to put in focus the essential, structural difference between American and English schools of education. That difference relates to models characterised as the 'market' and the 'monastery'. Within the market context, an institution can survive only by being competitive.

The rules of the competition are not set by graduate schools of education, and the rules cannot be altered by the schools. Moreover, the rules are powerful in two different fields of rivalry. A school of education can compete with another graduate professional school only insofar as it is linked with a powerful, organised, prestigious profession. In that sense its capacity to represent itself as a peer of medicine or law is directly limited by society's view of the status of teachers and other members of the educational profession. Similarly, its power to attract students of quality depends upon its reputation for demonstrated success in advancing the careers of these students. As long as attending the Waterend Law School brings assured financial and professional rewards, that law school will have the education school at a disadvantage.

The second field in which the rules of competition apply is the G.S.E.'s themselves. They depend upon national comparisons and ratings, which, in turn, are equally dependent upon scholarly achievement. The pursuit of these achievements leads to a modelling of the G.S.E.'s on the standards of research prevalent in arts and sciences and, by implication, to neglect of the more sharply professional functions of the school.

It follows, then, that G.S.E.'s are engaged in two separate but related competitions. The tragedy is that they can abstain from neither and yet have little hope of triumph in either. They will not take a place alongside the great schools of medicine and law, simply because teachers are not like lawyers or doctors. Nor will their university cousins in the arts and sciences finally accept them as equals; it will always be easier to do 'good work' in relatively pure research departments than in broadly-based professional schools which lack — indeed, never had — a clear mission.

To argue in these discouraging terms is not to imply that all is serene, either in other professional schools or in the arts and sciences. It is to assert only that the other constituencies — those, that is, of any size or significance — *feel* more secure within the context of most universities. A strong case can be made for the riposte that the sense of security in the arts and sciences is misplaced, that it would be better described as complacency. Another, different book would doubtless contrast the mission and commitment of schools of education with the self-indulgent academicism to be observed elsewhere in universities, often leading to the neglect of students themselves.

Within the G.S.E.'s I sense a prevailing mood of doubt and discomfort, succeeding some of the temporary enchantments of recent decades. Some critics argue that, during the years of expansion, the schools were careless in accepting new tasks and fresh money. They grew without having to confront disciplined questions about the proper nature of or limits to their expertise. The contraction of resources was correspondingly cruel, as was the abrupt sense that too much had been claimed for education, as well as too much for what its 'scientific' study could achieve. It is precisely this sharp decline that has driven G.S.E.'s back to a preoccupation with enrolments and heightened the contrasts between the aspirations of a scholarly faculty and the career-based needs of students.

The problem has surfaced. Some, however, would argue that the problem cannot be a serious one, on the grounds that it afflicts only a very small number of very special places, many of them private institutions, which do little harm and which stand at a great distance from the large, confident schools of education that produce the bulk of the nation's teachers. The G.S.E.'s in research universities can be safely ignored or treated as exotic birds of paradise. The real work goes on elsewhere.

I have rejected that comfortable conclusion, for a simple reason: G.S.E.'s exert an influence over attitudes and policies that bears no relationship to their size and number. They are widely respected as representing 'the best'; their *alumni* occupy positions of considerable power; less prestigious schools recruit from them key members of faculty; they seek to exert considerable influence on the national scene. For all these reasons they set the dominant values for all schools of education, however much they strive to throw around themselves a *cordon sanitaire*.

Whatever the strength of their protestations, just as they influence other schools, so they are directly affected by general opinion and public prejudice about the place of the teacher in society and the effectiveness of undergraduate programmes of teacher preparation. True, they have worked to separate themselves from both areas of infection. Undergraduate education, in the noblest of the G.S.E.'s, has either been abolished or is held warily at a distance. Similarly, the professional tasks of the school are defined in terms of the production of administrative or research personnel and not (understandably) of the developing competence of the professional teacher.

Against the background of the present argument, all this is readily understandable; indeed, it is irreproachable. As a policy of insulation, however, it cannot work. Those who teach in universities regard schools of education as a group or a class; some may be strong, some weak, but all are, in some sense, tarred with the same brush. There may, indeed, be no undergraduate teacher education at Waterend; but that is a highly unusual situation, and academics generally perceive G.S.E.'s as having a cumbersome entanglement in such work. That is what most of them have known in most places. In nearly all those places, undergraduate work is marked by the disfavour prevalent in Highside. Arts and sciences do not respect it, yet they cannot do without it; and the powerful men of the G.S.E. try unsuccessfully to pretend that undergraduate work isn't there.

The causes and consequences of such attitudes are clear. There has never been a strong, distinct tradition of teacher education; instead, teacher education passes as a function or even a by-product of a liberal undergraduate education. Little prestige attaches to the role of the teacher and correspondingly little to his or her education and training. That exercise becomes little more than a logistic base for more interesting and concentrated work at graduate level. Many who are teaching in arts and sciences regard education courses as a distraction for their abler students and freely doubt the value of the courses offered. Yet the very size of the enterprise makes it difficult to ignore; indeed, it generates resentment. Invariably, when G.S.E.'s respond to sullen disapproval by directing their interests in other and patently more scholarly directions, the same mandarins of arts and sciences equally resent this apparent desertion of the tasks of teacher training, not least because it pleases them to attribute to that desertion a decline in the standards of high schools and therefore in the quality of their freshmen.

How, then, can graduate schools of education succeed? In a competitive market, they are severely handicapped by the status of the profession with which they are concerned; also, they appear less robust than other major professional schools. At the same time, the G.S.E.'s are too large and pervasive to be relegated to the margins occupied by minor professional schools. If they seek to withdraw their presence from the undergraduate world, their detachment from what are seen as necessary if unglamorous tasks will be resented. If they strive to substitute for those tasks other tasks of conventionally higher quality, they invite comparison with other graduate professional schools or with graduate schools grounded in research and scholarship. Rarely if ever when such comparisons are made, in faculty clubs or elsewhere, are they to the credit or advantage of G.S.E.'s.

The reasons for this state of affairs may already be clear; but, as is evident in the preceding, brief analysis of the dilemmas derived from an undergraduate involvement, it may be helpful now to restate and reorder them.

The values of the G.S.E. remain unclear; nor are they readily compatible with one another. Perhaps the dominant impression left in my mind at the end of my visits and talks is one of institutions perpetually on the move — but not all in the same direction nor always with consistency, and not necessarily going anywhere. I have tried repeatedly to explain why I regard this unsettling phenomenon as explicable largely in terms of the way the system works and emphatically not in terms of some avoidable failure on the part of those who control the schools.

Traditionally, G.S.E.'s have been important engines for assisting the advancement of disadvantaged groups and societies. Women and blacks, for example, have made their way forward through such schools and reached better positions in society. It has been in education that such success was first achieved. There are obvious links between this phenomenon and the relatively modest standards of admission to such schools, which, in turn, have paid the penalty for their success. Previously disadvantaged groups now have good, if not equal, access to a range of other professions, and others have taken their place. The irony that lies near the surface is that schools of education, for as long as the status of the teacher remains modest, are *required* to be precisely where they are: at the base of the pyramid.

Similarly, as the educational professions are themselves stratified, the G.S.E.'s will want — and need — to concentrate on 'higher' tasks and functions. It is no accident or mistake that so many students pay, in time and money, to attend them in order to remove themselves from the classroom and the tasks of teaching. G.S.E.'s must therefore provide a variety of routes for such aspirants — into administration, research, curriculum development, employment in business. What is striking about such routes is that they are related by no unifying principle other than the negative one of leading away from teaching in any generally accepted sense. That's why so many G.S.E.'s must develop a latitudinarian policy — finding room and making provision for a bewildering variety of avenues. In doing that, however, they sacrifice focus and definition and back away from many of the immediate problems of schools.

I hope it has been sufficiently argued (for the benefit of the reader who is not an American) that G.S.E.'s could not survive without students and tuition and that their capacity to attract such commodities is directly dependent upon their reputation. That reputation can be derived only from scholarship and publication, and in pursuing such a reputation in those terms, the G.S.E. conveniently responds to the imperatives of its own university. Here, there appears to be a happy coincidence of two *desiderata,* to compete effectively in an open and cost-conscious market and to win academic esteem at home.

A price, however, has to be paid. Scholarship is valued above professionalism, and it becomes difficult to link scholarship with a unifying set of concerns — something that simply is not true of any other professional school of any size or stature. A clear priority is attached to winning for the G.S.E. able scholars of established reputation or certain promise, and questions about the nature of their interests or background experience inevitably are of secondary importance. If G.S.E.'s are latitudinarian, they are also atomistic, as more than one of their friends has observed. Those drawn in by a G.S.E. are given — and have every right to expect — an unusual degree of freedom in defining their interests and developing their work. For a G.S.E. under pressure or in decline, it is a short step to fall into intellectual anarchy.

More frequently, such dangers surface in milder forms. I have refered to these problems as relating to 'anchorage' and 'linkage'. There is little in decision-making at a G.S.E. to direct its effort unambiguously and continuously to the problems of teaching and schools. Given their nature, it is easier and more profitable to pursue less messy and more manageable research problems. I have argued above that these problems may be addressed in either a positivist or a universalist spirit, but that they are unlikely to be anchored in the concerns and needs of schools. Similarly, such 'new knowledge' as may by these processes be created is unlikely to find its way into practice; the institutional and intellectual links which should connect theory to practice are simply not there. (I doubt that such links exist in other countries, but that is another matter.) The G.S.E.'s incorporate no principle of continuity or stability, which, no doubt, is why one scholar drily remarked that each G.S.E. is always either dying or being subjected to artificial resuscitation.

The responsibilities of a dean in so perpetually critical a situation are awesome. No wonder some deans gaze wistfully with Dean Strong across the water at schools of law or business. A law school is unabashedly in the business of training lawyers, and it does so with an easy confidence. Nearly all of its faculty regard themselves as lawyers and practitioners, teaching is celebrated and rewarded, consultancy freely undertaken. There are few signs of dependence upon, still less of deference towards, 'outside' disciplines. The demand for places in the best schools and by the ablest students remains high.

These characteristics cannot, of course, simply be wished into the graduate schools of education. The dominant, even repetitive, argument of this book is that such courses of action are not open to them. Instead, the schools are obliged to oscillate, to borrow and import. Turning their backs upon, or their eyes away from, the professional education of teachers, they search vigorously for alternative missions. Others must judge of their success — their success as institutions, sharply differentiated from the brilliant achievements of those they have sheltered.

In this search they have surely not yet found autonomy or confidence or credibility in the world of education as a whole. Nor is it clear that they have won acceptance as full partners in the proud enterprise represented by the research universities. They have acknowledged the apparent necessity of responding to more narrowly defined academic imperatives. Now they move uneasily in the shadows between the graduate professional schools and the graduate schools of arts and sciences. It might seem that they have abandoned one base and not found another.

Was there — is there — no other way?

CHAPTER VII

A Letter from America

Following is the text of the letter Professor Rosencrantz wrote to me after reading the six preceding chapters.

I

It seems to me that in your Essay you make a number of fundamental errors and misperceive important aspects of the American educational scene. That is, I guess, only to be expected in a piece written by an outsider after a relatively brief series of visits and conversations. You are certainly right to abstain from "solutions" and "prescriptions." That is the proper business of American participants, and I shall try to contribute to it.

I still think, in spite of your explanations and protestations, that you are not entirely justified — some of us think not justified at all — in setting up two imagined universities and then constructing an impressionistic analysis of them. Although I would not go all the way with those among your critics who allege that you have invented the evidence in order to discover a puzzle, I do see their point. Indeed, from their point of view, you have now made things even worse by inventing me as well. But there would be serious logical problems if I now attempted to comment on that.

What disturbs me is that so many of the wise people known to both of us do, in fact, recognize the reality — I mean, of course, the verisimilitude — of the two portraits. By conflating the characteristics of many different places, so they allege, you have brought to the surface common underlying characteristics. It also disquiets me that those who have been emphatic in approval of your odd tactics of description have often been people close to, but not themselves inside, schools of education, or people known to be deeply anxious about what they see as a continuing failure of those famous schools.

But even if (and I would concede much of the argument here) the portraits do produce a nod or even a shudder of recognition, the fact remains that you have thrown away an opportunity to share with the reader some of the rich data you must by now have assembled about these places. Your failure to do so lays you wide open to the charge of being too polite, of being willing to strike but not to wound.

This is not just a matter of enjoying gossip, although most of us (like academics the world over) certainly do. What is missing, perhaps because you are simply not knowledgeable enough to see it, is a sense of particularity and of context. Obviously, there is a lot of Chicago in Waterend, with some sketchy gestures toward Berkeley and other places. So why not say so? What precisely do you gain, in the case of Highside, by dressing up Illinois in plumage borrowed from UCLA or Ohio State? Your argument is that you thereby gain "generality," but the price has been a heavy one. On this we can only disagree.

Before I seal the envelope containing this letter, I want to insist that writing as you have has landed you in the trap of setting up an insoluble problem. You seem to suppose that only one model of an excellent and fruitful school of education can exist and then only in some kind of utopian university. Also, I wish to argue that the strength of American diversity — which, like most Europeans, you understand so poorly — lies precisely in the development of a rich variety of institutional responses to some of the tensions you identified.

Meanwhile, you have not told us enough about real places. Let me illustrate. Nobody can understand the scene in Chicago without having a clear, if instinctive, sense of what it is to be "a Chicago professor." (How, by the way, would you feel if a Japanese observer confused Oxford and Manchester, as though they were merely two manifestations of the same phenomenon?) Chicago has a unique view of itself as a particular university. On the other hand, what is important in Chicago is that education is not a school but a department within a division of social sciences.

Harvard is another illustration. The deep changes there represented by the presidency of Eliot produced a climate in which graduate professional schools came to dominate much of the university's definition of its mission. Moreover, Harvard saw (and sees) its place in the academic world as one of elite leadership and benign but powerful political influence. Don't you see how these particular circumstances (which have little or no bearing in, for example, Teachers College, Columbia) create unique problems for a graduate school of education there? To be fair, you do allude to this problem more than once, but you persist in generalizing when particulars would be more illuminating.

My last example in concluding the first part of my charge against you must be from California, specifically the University of California. There, my argument is that UCLA is the way it is because Berkeley was — and is — Berkeley. During a long and sometimes colorful career, I have visited all the universities in the United States. I mean, of course, all the universities of which people like yourself would have heard. I have found none in which the celebration of academic excellence reaches the level it does across the bay from San Francisco. Naturally, I don't mean that Berkeley *is* academically "tops." It may or may not be, but that is beside the point. Its *mood* is what matters, its mood that makes life difficult perhaps for all professional schools and certainly for a school of education. You should have said so, and not left it to me.

Now, UCLA is a different matter. When it climbed rapidly to international renown, it pinned its name to the cultivation of graduate studies and professional schools, with medicine a notable example. Since it couldn't outsmart Berkeley, it took a different path. Do you suppose for one moment that in all these examples — Chicago, Harvard, Berkeley, and UCLA — the course of events and the possibility of improvement can be appreciated without paying attention to local detail? I don't think so.

I've said enough about my first charge, that you ignored the particular while searching for the general. That decision had its consequences. In the first place, for those who do not accept the broad lines of your analysis (and I am not among them), it is tempting to dismiss the evidence you offer as manufactured. But every reader must make his own mind up on that. Second, it diminishes your argument to disconnect schools of education from the universities they are part of and thus deprive the reader of useful information. Third, and for me most important, your Essay generates an undue sense of pessimism by accumulating a set of particular problems in one intractable puzzle. You appear to conclude that nothing can be done, that the problems lie in the structure. As an American, I am bound to think you're wrong, and I'll tell you why in Part III of this letter.

But first, I have some more criticisms.

II

As you will see, most of my criticisms are based on your failure to give full weight to the healthy opportunism of the American university, which obviously leads you to underestimate the capacity for change in a dynamic and diverse system. You don't see how much we have going for us — *us* being many of the people you met, sharing your doubts about present arrangements but not agreeing with all the elements in your analysis.

This failure on your part is surprising. In fact, it is glaring when viewed against the background of the market metaphor with which you play and in which I myself see a lot of force and relevance. Let me give three examples of how policy and performance in schools of education can be and are being affected by the particular circumstances of the market and its control.

The first way has to do with cash and its effect on research. There is no doubt — and you say so — that in the plushy days of the sixties and for a little while after, it was easy for schools of education to lay their hands on money. Priorities went where the money was. Faculty were recruited on a short- or a long-term basis to deliver the necessary work. Research assistants naturally congregated around the "in" projects. You are probably right in suggesting that many of those projects were diverted from the needs of schools and teachers, even if you sometimes exaggerate this point. A review of the work accomplished does show some neglect of the kind of work that might eventually be applied to the improvement of practices and policies.

You make the reasons for this clear enough. Obviously, they are related to the problems peculiar to being a graduate school of education in a research university. My point is that there is nothing total and immutable in this process. In Great Britain you speak and think as though the present economic recession will go on forever. In the United States we say, "*When* the recession ends. . . ." Suppose, then, that *when* present resources for research are again increased, the *objectives* of research are redefined. Suppose further, to take an argument you cherish, that those resources are applied to improving the education of teachers. (Note that I do not say "to the education of teachers in a research university.")

What would then happen is, I believe, already happening: the institutions you have been looking at would change. The social scientists may indeed have been running their own party. But lurking in the nooks and crannies of every good school of education are people willing and able to bend their talents in new directions. I shall have something to say later about those new directions. The point I am making here is that schools of education are not necessarily locked into the programs and agendas that you describe for them. You have looked neither far enough back nor far enough forward.

Money, then, is a factor in the market and its control. It is closely linked to the second factor — the power and personality of the dean. Again, you seem to have underestimated. Why? After all, you were among us when a dean of one of the greatest schools was being "evolved," and you know something of that discussion. Thus you should have realized that the "volatility" of the schools you refer to has a positive side. I refer to flexibility, to a capacity for change. With the arrival of a new dean, hiring policies change, the school begins to adapt its character, new missions are defined. You don't see such things happening in Europe.

Nor do you find a convincing analogy in Europe to the status and power of a university president. But you met several of them, and heard others speak of them. A president, especially a president in tune with a dean, can and does change policies. The president of Harvard has done so more than once. If schools of education are in bad shape — and they are — it is partly because university presidents haven't taken enough notice of them, or have allowed them to deteriorate into confusion. You describe the performance of a provost at Highside; we take such people seriously.

These, then, are three factors that could break the claustrophobic symmetry of the trap you describe: money, to tune the research agenda; the personality and policies of a dean; the priorities of a president. You will understand why I have pressed these criticisms on you, alongside those in Part I of my letter. Taken together, they amount to an indictment of the rigidity of your method. I am taking the trouble to point out your error because I believe that, on the whole, your analysis is sound, and I wish to urge on your readers that something — more properly, *some things* — can be done about it.

Before I specify those things, I must explain, as an American inside the system, why (in spite of the harsh and justified criticisms) I accept much of your analysis and wish to turn it around, into an argument for reform.

III

What do I mean by stating my agreement with your analysis?

I mean that I recognize the trap into which these particular schools of education have fallen. With you, I doubt whether there is all that much any of them could have done to avoid it. Professional schools in our universities *do* reflect the prestige of the professions for which they offer training and credentials. There is no need to underline your reasons for arguing that schools of education would, for that reason alone, be in considerable difficulty.

Since, for that reason, they cannot achieve the autonomy or dignity of medicine or law, they seek another source of authority and acceptance. They — I mean the schools most visible and most respected for their scholarship — have tuned in to the values and habits of the graduate schools of arts and sciences, especially the social sciences. In the end, however, that doesn't help them. They remain professional schools aspiring to another status — and the more they aspire, the more they are likely to alienate themselves from the world of schools and education. As a colleague observed grimly to me the other day: ''We can't dance any faster, but we're dancing to the wrong music.'' In the end they, like the rest of us, remain dependent on the market and the quality of the tuition-paying students they can attract. And *that* is precisely the problem.

I agree, too, that schools of education represent a continuous spectrum of activity and reputation. I do not believe that those in research universities can be treated in splendid isolation. They solve no problems by asserting, as they so often do, their ''difference'' from the ordinary run of such schools. One of my friends here, not renowned for an excess of modesty, regularly observes: ''I don't often walk with professors of education.'' Attention should therefore be directed to what another of your correspondents has characterized as reciprocal infection. The most renowned graduate schools are the bubbling source of educational fads, and they exercise a disproportionate influence on the media, foundations, government, and public opinion. Moreover, their alumni are often well placed on the faculties of other, lesser universities, to which they bring the same values. Chicago and Stanford are admired for what they are believed to have done. Whatever you may have been told in private, in public their deans and professors are listened to in collective awe. The same is true of Harvard, as readers of the *New York Times* know well.

But this is not a one-way process. However hard they may wriggle, schools of education remain just that: schools of education. They are associated, especially but by no means exclusively in the minds of other academics, with the ill-regarded business of teacher education. They may be guilty of little or none of that prejudice themselves, but that isn't the point. They remain leaders of a poor and motley bunch known to attract only the weaker students. The more strenuously the leading schools disown the run-of-the-mill places, the more annoyance they cause in and out of universities by their desertion of the causes of public schooling in the pursuit of easier options.

Make no mistake about it: there is in this country a crisis of confidence in the public schools and of the teachers who are so widely blamed for the poor state of the schools. You touched on some of the roots of this, but you underestimate its extent and depth. Far from sharing your pessimistic view, I believe that this widespread anxiety could and should be a powerful force for change, in which some (not all) schools of education will have a key role. I have already explained why, given the aggressive pragmatism of American universities, I believe change is now possible and will be possible for the foreseeable future. If public concern about schooling is turned toward the improvement of teacher education and pedagogy in general, certain desirable consequences will follow.

What's more, there never was, nor will be, a better time to undertake such changes. For many years, in this country as in yours and others, the overriding preoccupation was to provide — no matter how — teachers in vast numbers to deal with ever-rising enrollments. Quantity was all that mattered; quality was nowhere to be seen. Universities and colleges became factories producing teachers. For demographic and other reasons, those hectic years are past. Enrollment is down, small institutions are threatened, pressure has been relaxed, at least for awhile. Enrollment in teacher-education courses has fallen by half since 1973. The time is ripe for change. Schools of education should — in research universities and elsewhere — seize the opportunity. What they should not do, of course, is keep their backs turned on this question while cultivating a mandarinlike detachment from public schooling.

Most of us are smart enough to see that national interests will be served by a new concern with the quality of teachers. The gap now opening up between the complex needs of industry and what we believe our public schools can deliver is of dizzying proportions. Who is going to teach in our high schools? Even if educational standards remain static, we will still have a problem. Don't suppose that we are unaware of what our competitors are achieving or unmindful of the threat posed by international competition. We know only too well what happened to England.

Let me put it another way. In my view, we are close to the national mood that followed the launching of Sputnik I. It makes little difference that this time the threat is economic rather than military. What has made the difference is that, I must confess to my surprise and chagrin, last time around little attention was paid to the problem of teacher quality — partly, perhaps, because we were in a hurry and were still preoccupied with the logistics of supplying teachers. This time it could be different. If enough people take notice, there will be a general, effective concern with the quality of teaching.

You are right, of course, to insist that society gets the teachers it deserves, that society won't get better ones until it values them more highly. You are right, too, to stress the debilitating dependence of teachers on local politicians and pressure groups. Finally, you are right to hint at the damage already done to teaching and learning by the indiscriminate widening of the frontiers of educational ambition. Today, altogether too much is expected of schools. But these things may change too, especially if the schools of education address themselves to changes that lie within their power.

If the vicious circle is to be snapped, it must be broken in more than one place.

Please don't make the mistake of supposing that in some way all graduate schools of education either now have, or should have under some different dispensation, the same set of functions, the same mission. I have already drawn attention to your errors in that area. No. The schools examined (but not specified by you) differ sharply from each other, partly by choice and partly because of the institutional context in which each school resides. There can be few "rules" governing their development. As a group they should offer a variety of models of what it is to "succeed" as graduate schools of education in research universities. Stanford is never going to be "like" Teachers College, Columbia. A wise dean pays attention to the restraints on and opportunities of his university. He does not ignore the policies of the university's president. He brings to his task a personal (and rarely secret) list of things he wants to get done.

But I hope that, much more than in the recent past, this dean will be more in tune with the tasks and problems of all schools and colleges of education — not, I say again, that the dean will wish to be like all of them. On the contrary, our dean should believe that most of them should be closed. Teacher education of one sort or another is conducted at nearly 1,400 colleges and universities. The first requirement of any coalition for reform would be that many of them should be shut down; I mean, of course, the teacher-education programs, not necessarily the entire institution.

The reasons for this essential first step are simple and obvious, even if our only concern is to improve the position of the best graduate schools. The base for teacher education and serious educational study is simply too wide and uneven. In a world where "anything goes," and it often has, professional standards and scholarly achievement will not be taken seriously. That was the position with medical schools until Flexner set about them with his scalpel. I don't believe that a similar job of amputation can be accomplished in education; nor do I think that the necessary millions are available to achieve the preeminent superiority of those places left on the scene. Something closer to the amelioration of law schools might be envisaged — a reduction in number, still leaving a long and flexible hierarchy of quality and reputation. But it would be a continuous hierarchy, in a way not now true of education. Of course, everybody knows that the law schools at Harvard or Berkeley are not in the same class as that at———————. Well, perhaps infected by your own reticence, I had better not mention it. The latter place, though cheaper and nastier, is acknowledged to be in the same *business* as its big brothers.

If the first requirement is a reduction in numbers and some consequent assimilation of type in schools of education, the second requirement is an accelerating change in the patterns of teacher education. You are right when you say that you met no defenders of the present arrangements. That's because there are none.

We Americans have — uncharacteristically — taken too much for granted the dismal state of undergraduate teacher education. People here will agree with what you say about it, and some will point to encouraging developments. At the University of Washington at Seattle, for example, 40 percent of students in education programs already have the bachelor's degree when they enter the university. This may prove, on examination, to be not all that unusual. For some time, California has required a fifth year for those wishing to be teachers. There is considerable interest in extended programs, and you draw attention to the recent work of Bunnie Smith.

All this should be consolidated and carried a step further. Of course, nothing will be achieved overnight; no single agency in Washington or the state capitals or the universities or the teachers' unions has enough power for that. Nevertheless, what is needed is a firm and unambiguous view that teacher education and training should be for graduates only. I suppose that — reluctantly, in my case — we shall have to swallow some ''preprofessional courses in education'' for undergraduates, but let's not make too much of them. A change of that magnitude would, leaving all else aside, give schools of education a clearer structure as professional schools. At present, they are in a terrible quandary: Are they in the business of undergraduate education (tramping about with arts and science), or are they in the business of teacher education?

Under such circumstances I should hope that many G.S.E.'s would move back into the field of teacher education. I don't know about Harvard, but I would be surprised if Stanford did not take such an opportunity to strengthen its present commitment. These are among the leading institutions. If they don't declare an interest, it is difficult to see why their ''followers'' should bother. You must take seriously what I said about the threat to national prosperity and security posed by the collapse of quality teaching in public schools. In numerical terms the contribution of a few leading G.S.E.'s would be a modest one. But, drawing even a sprinkling of able undergraduates from such places into the public service of teaching would have powerful symbolic force.

That brings me to what you say about anchorage and linkage. The support of graduate teacher-training programs by foundations and others will bring new people and new ideas into the G.S.E.'s. It will make clear, if we don't already know it, that we have little notion of how to train these or other teachers. Research will be anchored in such alarmingly fundamental questions, at the expense of some of the easier or peripheral inquiries which you group under the heading ''imperialism.'' It sounds harsh and narrow, but schools of education need, first and foremost, to be schools of pedagogy — and good ones, at that.

I think that, at least in part, is what you should mean by *anchorage*. But even the performance of elegant work on relevant questions is not, by itself, enough. G.S.E.'s (I mean throughout those in research universities, in your sense) must exercise leverage and influence on other schools of education, most of which will be deeply involved in the preparation of teachers. The G.S.E. must lead in *this;* it must be preeminent among the schools of pedagogy. That is to say, there must be ''linkage,'' and the engagement of G.S.E.'s in teacher preparation is an effective way of achieving that goal.

Still, it need not be the only way, and it might be an indispensable way. I have merely argued that, in terms of institutional politics, G.S.E.'s are more likely to be kept on what I regard as the right course if they do have such an engagement. But not all will, or could. The oversimplified vision I am offering for your encouragement depends in large measure on the elevation of all programs of teacher preparation to the graduate level. That may not happen. Some G.S.E.'s — and I repeat that they need not, must not, look and be alike — will take the view that other places are honestly better at the business than they are — a large public university, for example.

It is the principle that endures: G.S.E.'s must lead the schools of education, not stumble about trying to follow somebody else. They can do that by distinguished, innovative work in graduate teacher training or by undertaking the kind of effort typified by the Institute for Research in Teaching at Michigan State. But it would be wrong to take so narrow-minded a view as to equate schoolteaching with education or even to suppose that the only way to take the first seriously is to personally engage in the everyday tasks of teacher preparation. *That* is one way to demonstrate that you are taking practitioners seriously.

But there are other ways; there must be. In each G.S.E. you visited there were some faculty — apparently only a handful, often isolated — with a strong interest in schools and teachers. What I have said about the pragmatism of American universities should have convinced you that such small groups, nourished by public concern and funds, could become the core of a new influence. The trick is knowing who they are and how to influence them.

Where we are in agreement, I suppose, is in our belief that G.S.E.'s have painted themselves into a corner or that they have had it done to them. I believe that some, but not all, G.S.E.'s can and should get into a ''better space.'' Apparently, you believe that they are all caught in the same place.

So far, in seeking to moderate your gloomy view, I have argued that American universities are much more adaptable than you give them credit for being, and that things might therefore change. I have attacked you for lumping all G.S.E.'s together, an error compounded by the invention of two far-from-ideal types, and then supposing that they must all endure the same fate. I reply that we do have and need multiple models and that every example is a special one. Then, it seems, I move back into rough agreement with you on why and how many G.S.E.'s got into their current hypnotized state, by ''failing'' to be a professional school like law, by ''trying'' to disconnect them-selves both from public schooling and (worse in a way) from the whole sector of schools of education which they should be leading, by ''aspiring'' to be more like a graduate school of arts and sciences while encumbered with an inferior student body.

I was not content to rest there, however, and have now gone on to argue for two general reforms, which could be combined to place G.S.E.'s where they belong. The first is a dramatic reduction in the overall number of teacher-training institutions and a concentration of excellence and resources. The second is the dignifying of teacher education by making it an entirely graduate activity.

To say that all this could happen is not to assert that it will. Even if it did, my pluralism would keep me from suggesting that all G.S.E.'s approach the kind of model I have sketched for you. So there are alternatives to be found. Just what these alternatives are will depend on particular circumstances, but I am not very hopeful about what can be achieved without the two major reforms I stipulated. I certainly do not believe that G.S.E.'s will cheerfully survive if they cling to the present implicit definition of their purpose in the present context of universities as they are and teacher training as it is.

Two or three useful possibilities occur to me, however. They are possibilities in the reformed world I envisage as much as in the unre-formable world your analysis implies. Each implies the dissolution of the G.S.E. as we know it, so that, if I do not take care, I may be saying that these schools can survive only if they are destroyed. Certainly, their frontiers will have to be weakened and they will have to abandon the irrelevant pretensions of a professional school.

Let me explain. It is not absurd to claim that it is the business of the whole university, not just of one specialized part of it, to educate and train teachers. If the graduate-only model does not prevail, then the best hope for some schools of education (certainly in research universities) may be to seek an effective merger with arts and sciences, to become, if you will, a department within them. Certainly they cannot succeed on the outside.

Similarly, the *education enterprise* (and I deliberately choose this loose phrasing) might in some places move from being a minor professional school of uncertain purpose to the entrepreneur or broker for an entire campus. You have, I think, little or no sense of how much goodwill and expertise is lying around on campus waiting to be mobilized, ready to be applied to public schooling. Here is a task for a school of education, whatever it may then be called. At the University of California at Berkeley, attested by a carefully prepared and published list, some fifty-six projects are being directed at elementary and secondary schooling. Only eight have any connection with the university's school of education. It is absurd that this should be so.

A third possibility for the graduate schools of education in research universities is that, again, they should abandon their professional school functions and become research institutes. I mean only that a few might do this. It is wrong that so many schools should remain in the business of generating degrees at the Master's and Doctor's levels when the interests of the faculty lie along lines of research having little bearing on the diurnal tasks of teaching in such a school. At a time when job opportunities are contracting, I note that not a few of my colleagues have a bad conscience about this.

So much for my three examples, which I put alongside my major reforms, either as complements or as alternatives. The package I described above does, you will agree, amount to a newly defined mission for the G.S.E. You are right in supposing that the G.S.E. needs such a mission.

I would like to close as I began, by reasserting the accessibility of change, a change in the structures themselves if you wish. The earlier part of my argument turned on the power of enlightened self-interest and the urgency of linking the graduate schools of education to the imperatives of producing better teachers.

Because I find such a note wholly lacking in your Essay, let me place alongside that energetic pragmatism another powerful consideration. I am confident that among the young, but not among only them, there is a deep well of idealism ready to be tapped. It may be that you brought the detachment of the Old World to the writing of your Essay; you certainly brought not a little of its cynicism. There would be massive support in this country for a regeneration of the schools of education, led by the graduate schools of education, drawing in more able and dedicated graduates as teachers. We certainly need them. I hope that arguments like yours might lead to a reassertion of just that sense of mission. Whatever you say, that is why some of our best people are in the graduate schools of education today.

I hope, too, that we shall keep our discussion alive.

Yours sincerely,

Benedict Rosencrantz

Acknowledgments and Sources

Most books owe a great deal to those who are thanked in a note of this kind. This short book owes everything to them.

The text itself should make this clear, as all the observations and comments in it are derived from a long series of conversations with those I now wish to name. I know that many of them will not accept such conclusions as are drawn or implied, but they will agree that such errors of judgement are entirely mine. No one could have better or more generous counsellors. I therefore wish to thank the following persons (whose professional affiliations as given here were current when the study was conducted):

IN CALIFORNIA

At the Hewlett Foundation

President Robert W. Heyns (formerly president of the University of Michigan and chancellor at the University of California, Berkeley).

At the Hoover Institution

James G. March, senior fellow.

At Stanford University

Martin J. Evans, associate dean, humanities and sciences; Arthur P. Coladarci, dean of the Graduate School of Education, and his assistant, Valerie Familant;

Professors Robert C. Calfee, Lee J. Cronbach, Elliot W. Eisner, Michael W. Kirst, Lewis B. Mayhew, Decker F. Walker, and Hans N. Weiler.

At the University of California, Berkeley

The successive chancellors Albert H. Bowker and Ira M. Heyman;

In the Center for the Study of Higher Education, Sheldon Rothblatt, Janet Ruyle, and Martin A. Trow;

In the School of Education, acting deans Geraldine J. Clifford and Dale Tillery, and Professor James L. Jarrett;

In the Law School, Professors John E. Coons, Robert H. Mnookin, and Stephen D. Sugarman;

In the School of Public Policy, Professor David L. Kirp;

In the School of Journalism, Professor David Littlejohn.

At the University of California, Los Angeles

Vice-Chancellor Charles Z. Wilson;

In the School of Education, Dean John I. Goodlad and his assistant, Arthur Berchin;

Professors Lawrence W. Erickson, C. Wayne Gordon, Evan R. Keislar, Thomas J. LaBelle, Laura M. Pope, Kenneth Sirotnik, Rodney W. Skager, and Robert Wenkert.

IN ILLINOIS

At The Spencer Foundation

President H. Thomas James.

At the University of Chicago

Former president John T. Wilson;

In the Department of Education, Chairman Charles E. Bidwell and his assistant, Linda Budd;

Professors C. Arnold Anderson, Benjamin S. Bloom, John E. Craig, Jacob W. Getzels, George Hillocks, Jr., Philip Jackson, Marie T. Jones, Zalman Usiskin, Charles Wagener, Harold S. Wechsler, and Douglas M. Windham.

At the University of Illinois, Champaign-Urbana

President John E. Corbally, Jr., Chancellor William Gerberding, and Vice-Chancellors Edwin L. Goldwasser and Morton W. Weir;

In the College of Education, Dean J. Myron Atkin;

Professors Richard C. Anderson, C. Benjamin Cox, Terry Denny, Lilian G. Katz, Alan Peshkin, James D. Raths, and Robert E. Stake.

IN MASSACHUSETTS

In the Cambridge Rindge and Latin School

Headmaster Edward Sarasin and Dr. Diane Tabor.

At The Commission on Educational Issues

Director Arthur G. Powell.

At Harvard University

President Derek C. Bok;

In the Graduate School of Education, Dean Paul N. Ylvisaker, Associate Dean Blenda J. Wilson, Assistant Dean Ursula Wagener, former deans Francis Keppel and Theodore R. Sizer;

Professors Stephen K. Bailey, Mary Jo Bane, Roland S. Barth, Arthur S. Bolster, Courtney B. Cazden, Richard P. Chait, David K. Cohen, Joseph L. Featherstone, Nathan Glazer, Patricia A. Graham, Jerome T. Murphy, and Ronald G. Slaby;

In the Business School, Professor James Haskett;

In the Divinity School, Dean George E. Rupp;

In the Law School, Dean Albert M. Sacks, Assistant Dean Russell A. Simpson, and Professor Paul A. Freund;

In the Department of Psychology, Professors Jerome Bruner and Sheldon H. White.

At Massachusetts Institute of Technology

In the Division for Study and Research in Education, Director Benson R. Snyder, Associate Director Barbara S. Nelson, and Professor Judah L. Schwartz.

At Salem State College

President James T. Amsler;

Professors Stephen J. Clarke, Nancy D. Harrington, and Vincent L. Hawes.

Others

Dr. Gregory Anrig, state commissioner of education; Dr. Aaron Fink, superintendent of schools, Newton, Massachusetts; Dr. Edwin D. Campbell, president, Gulf Management Institute.

IN MICHIGAN

At Michigan State University

President Edgar L. Hardin and Provost Clarence L. Winder;

In the College of Education, Dean Judith E. Lanier and Professor Lee Shulman.

IN NEW YORK

At the Ford Foundation, Harold Howe II, vice-president for education and public policy, and Program Officer Edward J. Meade, Jr.

ACKNOWLEDGMENTS AND SOURCES

At Teachers College, Columbia University

President Lawrence A. Cremin and Dean Harold J. Noah;

Professors Arno A. Bellack, Leonard S. Blackman, Morton Deutsch, Ellen Lagerman, Hope J. Leichter, Dale Mann, Richard Vigilante, and Sloan R. Wayland.

IN OHIO

At Ohio State University

Professors Donald P. Anderson, Jack A. Culbertson, Luvern L. Cunningham, Frederick R. Cyphert, Martha L. King, Kevin A. Ryan, Russell J. Spillman, and Nancy E. Zimpher.

IN WASHINGTON STATE

At the University of Washington

James I. Doi, dean of the College of Education;

Professors Charles O. Burgess, Theodore Kaltsounis, Donna H. Kerr, David L. Madsen, Timothy Trandal, and Robert E. Tostberg.

IN WASHINGTON, D.C.

Rep. John Brademas.

At the American Association of Colleges of Teacher Education

David G. Imig, executive director, and Karl Massanari, associate director.

At the National Education Association

Drs. Robert M. McClure, Bernard H. McKenna, and William Mondale.

Some debts in particular must be emphasised. Valerie Clark produced with immaculate skill successive drafts of this book, as well as the long "Chronicle" from which it is derived. Only a handful of correspondents will know what is involved in deciphering over 100,000 words of my handwriting. David Littlejohn of the School of Journalism at Berkeley was my most ferocious but industrious critic. Martin Trow, also at Berkeley, offered me amusement, encouragement, and advice matched only by the support of Barbara Scott Nelson and Ben Snyder at MIT. Jerome Bruner will recognise echoes of numerous conversations extending over ten years in Oxford and Harvard. He already knows how much I owe him. Ed Meade at the Ford Foundation in New York had the idea in the first place; so it must be an open question whether any thanks are due to him. I, of course, think that they are.

Oxford
June 1981

Designed by Elizabeth Finger
Produced by Publishing Center for Cultural Resources